Watch Out for Bears

An Adventure in Leadership

Dan Kellogg

BOOK PUBLISHERS NETWORK
Changing the World One Book at a Time

Book Publishers Network
P.O. Box 2256
Bothell • WA • 98041
Ph • 425-483-3040
www.bookpublishersnetwork.com

10 9 8 7 6 5 4 3 2 1

Printed in the United States of America

LCCN   2014908775
ISBN   978-1-940598-38-3

Editor: Kira Hagenbuch Monica/Julie Scandora
Cover Designer: Adrian Sims
Book Designer: Melissa Vail Coffman

All quoted Scripture from
New Living Translation,
Tyndale House Publishers

This book is dedicated to my grandpa, Ralph Kellogg, who taught me to love to hunt and to love Christ; to my parents, Don and Margaret Kellogg, who always encouraged my adventures; and to my wife, Audrey, and my children, Kristen Dickison and Daniel Kellogg, who have been at my side and willing to let me lead them into adventure.

Contents

Foreword

In the middle of the night on a hiking trip with my parents, I woke up to the sound of heavy footsteps and loud grunting sounds. I was sure there was a bear outside my tent. Around the campfire the night before, my dad had read stories of real-life bear attacks. Just before bed, he had mentioned seeing a bear in that very area a couple of years before. Those were the thoughts running through my mind. I have never been as scared in my life as I was that night. I was paralyzed with fear, in cold feverish sweats, lying there, imagining the bear rising up on his hind legs trying to get at the food we had hung in the tree. He was coming for us next. I was able to wake my mother, and she too was scared. After what seemed like hours, the sound went away, and we were able to fall back asleep. In the morning, I told everyone the story of what I had heard. After some investigation, it turned out a deer had come into our camp and dug a hole near my tent—the grunting sounds had just been my dad snoring.

Growing up with Dan Kellogg as your father meant you had moments like that night where you were out in a wilderness situation, scared for your life. My dad could turn any boring old hike into a survival situation by taking short cuts, misreading the difficulty of the hike on a map, or telling stories to get my imagination to run wild. And yet, my best memories growing up were the times spent on adventure outings with my dad.

From the time I was about nine to age eighteen, my dad and I would go with other dads and their kids on yearly trips to Montana. We stayed in tents, dug our own bathrooms, went on overnight hiking trips, fly fished, and cooked food over Coleman stoves. On these trips, I learned about experiencing life in the wild, snipe hunts, and that when your mom is not around you get to do dangerous things, like jumping off a bridge into a river. One year, all my dad brought for us to eat was deer meat, and as a teenage girl, deer meat was not something I particularly liked. But, I learned that when you don't have any other options, deer meat looks pretty good. I still treasure those trips with my dad, and I am proud to be a woman that can tough it out in the wild.

My dad not only taught me about surviving in the wild, but he also taught me how to follow Jesus Christ. He was—and is—a great role model for actually living out your faith. I have come to realize that your family knows the true you. You can put on a face to other people, but at home and with your family, your true self and true nature are revealed. So who is the real Dan Kellogg? He genuinely loves Jesus, loves the outdoors, is full of wisdom, loves our family, cares deeply about our church, is great in a crisis, and so much more. He is also human and has his quirks, like being super competitive, has occasional gear envy, and has been known to cheat occasionally in family card games. I have listened to my dad's sermons for thirty years now, and his teachings on the Bible never get old. He has a way of looking through the Scripture to find the story behind the words and provides a different viewpoint or a deeper meaning.

In this book, my dad makes the Scripture come alive in his teaching on the Pharisees and Jesus. You will get a chance to reflect on the type of Pharisees you might encounter in your life, as well as how to watch out for them. You will also get to hear some of my dad's wild adventure stories of encountering bears. If you love the outdoors and stories about bears and would love to learn more about Jesus, then this is the book for you.

I am proud to be my dad's daughter and I hope his teaching and stories bring as much joy and insight to your life as they have to mine.

Kristen Dickison

Growing up, I thought all dads were adventurous, tough, fearless, spiritual, and willing to face their fears. If only this were the case. When I was a child, my dad would tell me how following Jesus could cost him his life and that it might not go well for him. Living for Jesus, as tough as it is, was worth it for him. I believe these conversations helped me see the true gospel. These conversations helped me to see my relationship with Jesus as a dangerous wilderness adventure. Many Christian men today write books that are about adventure, but when you watch a video of the author, it is almost comical how quickly their sweater vest and vegetarian appetite make their tough book seem like all talk. My dad breaks the standard Christian writer mold. This book illustrates real fear-covered man adventures that will draw you to adventure, away from your tan khakis, and into the life Jesus is calling you to.

My dad and I have encountered bears many times while hunting and camping. Some people tend to run screaming. I have never seen my dad run from a bear. (I wish I could say the same about myself!) Fifteen years ago, I jumped head first into ministry. I have grown to realize that some of the most challenging bears my dad has faced were not in some Artic Circle caribou hunt, not near the river on a Montana fly-fishing trip or even on a Washington State high hunt. No, some of the most challenging bears my dad has faced have been during his adventure in leadership in the church. They have left wounds and scars that my dad never showed to us kids until later in life. Looking back, I'm glad I didn't know! I'm glad my dad faced them. The question is: what will *you* do with these bears? I believe every minister has a "church bear" story of people standing against what Jesus is doing in their ministry. Some ministers don't make it. Some quit while they are at their most impactful moment of ministry. My dad will inspire you to move from giving up and living in hurt and self-loathing to hearing Jesus calling you to an adventure again. He will define some of the ugliest and most dangerous enemies the church has, the Pharisees. My dad will help you see how Jesus dealt with the Pharisees—even if that Pharisee is you.

Here is a story that illustrates the theme of this book and my dad's character. During a junior high school wrestling match, I was temporarily injured by an illegal move by my opponent, which resulted in me winning the match. Afterwards, the boy's dad (a large, angry man) decided to take his anger out on my dad. My dad didn't back down. This book doesn't back down either. It doesn't bend or dance around. This book is for real followers of Christ who have to encounter bears. These bears are people who cling to their dead structures and systems—people who would kill you to keep them in place. It is for believers who have traded their adventurous relationship with Jesus for self-dignity. People like you and me.

Before you start to dive into this book, beware: it might be talking about people like you. This book is not baby blue and fluffy with the adventure taken out to keep from offending bears. This book is all about Jesus! The bears are unavoidable. Let's start this conversation!

Thank you, Dad, for being. You are my Gladiator, my Braveheart, and my hero, and to this day I have never seen a better dad than you!

Daniel Kellogg

Introduction

It was the summer of 1968. My mom and dad had rented a cabin just outside of town in Stehekin, Washington, a small town accessible only by boat. They took my sister, brothers, and me there, to the edge of the wilderness, for vacation. There was not much in the way of entertainment, but families traveled there because it was secluded and away from the bustle of everyday life. As a young boy, I'd heard many stories about bears, which had made me very afraid of them. I didn't like reading much, but I couldn't put down a good bear story. I'd read a lot about them: adventure stories that ended in bear attack, articles about maulings that left people disfigured, and newspaper clippings of people who'd lost their lives to vicious bears. I'd also listened to my grandpa tell stories of his bear encounters. So by twelve years old, I already had a fear of them.

When we got to Stehekin, we rented a 1940 Plymouth sedan by the mile. When driven backwards, the sedan erased the miles, so my frugal dad drove it in reverse—a lot. Upon arrival, we got a bit bored, so we asked some of the locals what we could do for fun. They encouraged us to watch the bears that came out in the evenings to dig for food in the town dump. I told my dad I was in for this: I was finally ready for my own bear encounter. We decided to drive out to the village dump. Backwards.

When we got to the dump, we were not alone—several cars were lined up to watch the bears. The sun started to set. Crows perched in the trees. There was a fresh pile of garbage from the locals for the bears to dig through. Bears started to move in and feed for the evening meal. We were ready for them.

The first bear I saw walked right by my car window. He was less than three feet from my face. My heart raced, my legs stiffened, and my body filled with adrenaline—the bear was even bigger and more dangerous than I'd imagined. I saw up-close his arm muscles and his long, sharp claws that dug into the ground as he walked. I watched the bear move to the pile and saw the sheer power of his ability to dig. His strength reminded me of a small backhoe.

The bears were five to six feet long, three feet at the shoulders. Some of them topped five hundred pounds. As they rose up on their hind legs, they easily towered over our car. I thought I'd feel safe in the car, but I didn't. I felt intimidated. I thought that if they placed their paws on my window, they might be able to push it in and have some fresh meat. When they looked in our direction, it was as if they were looking right into my eyes. *Do they think I look tasty?* I wondered. The adrenaline I experienced was awesome. I felt so alive!

After observing them for a couple of hours, I became desensitized by their presence. They appeared harmless. I started to feel comfortable around them. My fears diminished. Soon, I disregarded the predatory nature of these wild animals. I forgot about their capabilities. I ignored what would happen if they chose to attack.

The next day, filled with self-assurance, my brother Ron and I hiked back to the dump without our parents' permission or knowledge. We wanted to watch the bears at eye level. We planned to sneak up within a few feet and experience them without the safety of the car. Once there, we noticed a mother black bear with her cubs, digging for a meal in the garbage. I felt invincible to be out in the open—alone—with these animals. Watching an animal that close heightens the senses. I felt the wind in my face and heard every little sound. I could even hear the bear chewing through its latest find. This little trip lit up the flame of adventure in my soul.

Up until that moment, we could see the bears, but they didn't see us. Quietly and slowly, we walked closer and closer to them. We were careful not to make a sound; even our breathing was quiet. Every muscle tensed. I actually smelled the air to see if I could catch their scent. We were within fifty yards. I looked at my brother. He looked back. We decided to do something only a couple of crazy kids would do: we charged, yelling as we approached. We wanted to see the bears' reaction. We caught them completely off guard. *What do they think we are?* I wondered. Completely startled, the bears moved quickly away from the racket. All three hastily climbed different trees with unbelievable speed, tearing bark off them as they scrambled to get away from two crazed kids.

We stood at the bottom of the trees, laughing hysterically at the bears. It was the most fun we'd had on our vacation. But things can change suddenly. And they did. It became a life-altering experience.

The mother bear huffed loudly and angrily snapped her jaw from thirty feet up in the tree. She stared at us, waving her head back and forth. We didn't recognize those signals of agitation. We just laughed even more. The mother bear couldn't take it anymore. She made her move and started coming down the tree. I could hear the bear's claws shredding the bark as she quickly descended the trunk. Laughter turned to fear. I started to realize that it wasn't going to end well. I feared for my life—so did my brother. This wasn't the same docile creature I'd watched feeding; she'd decided to defend her cubs. She headed straight for us.

We were in trouble. I was twelve. My brother was fourteen. Our lack of experience and overconfidence got us in this situation. We had forgotten all the stories about how dangerous bears can be.

As soon as she reached the ground, we turned and ran as fast as we could. The thick brush had no trail, so we made our own. I remembered that a bear could travel at thirty miles per hour in short bursts—there was no way to outrun her. One swipe of her paw could open me up. Her jaw could break every bone in my body. If she wanted to kill me, there wasn't much I could do about it. We really shouldn't have run because we looked like prey. But we ran anyway, making our own trail through the bushes and trees. My brother ran right into, and through, a bees' nest. He was stung repeatedly but kept running. I somehow managed to avoid the cloud of bees altogether. Scared of being torn to shreds or eaten, I looked over my shoulder as often as possible to see if the bear was behind us. It was the most scared I'd been in my entire life. Thankfully, the bear didn't chase us down and give us what we deserved.

I would never again look at a mother bear with cubs as completely harmless.

THE ADVENTURE BEGINS

The life of following Jesus is an adventure in leadership. The level of leadership you rise to will directly relate to the level of pain you can endure. This adventure is not for everyone. Many people want to say they follow Christ but never really follow Him into their leadership adventure. He has a path—and an adventure—that is unique to each of us.

If you choose to follow, the path will lead to some very dangerous people. Like the mother bear, they can seem harmless and even docile. But they will do whatever it takes to protect their ways of life. They are not who you'd think, either. They are not from another religion. They are not outsiders. They take us by surprise. They are the religious who think that life is about what we can't do, instead of who we can become. They are the Pharisees. They look at the Bible as a weapon to beat others with, instead of as a mirror to help themselves. Their way of life is the measuring stick. If we don't live up to it, we'd better be prepared to fight. To know how to handle these religious people, we will have to follow the example of Jesus. We need to stand up to them and confront them in order to stay close on our path.

The Pharisees from the New Testament were protecting their religious ways of life. Their religion had become a game. They taught that if we followed their rules, we would win. Jesus was always breaking their rules and raising the bar. He taught us how to confront these Pharisees. He did it not with a checklist or instructions but through His encounters with them and in the way He lived his life. Jesus gave His life to break the power of those Pharisees. He calls us to give our lives to do the same.

In this book, you will find four things in each chapter. First, I tell a bear story. I love the outdoors and the unexpected danger that comes with it. These bear stories relate to the dangerous encounters that will be a part of our lives as we follow Jesus. Second, I teach you about the Pharisees and their interactions with Jesus. Along the way, we learn why they were so dangerous. Through Jesus, we also learn how to handle these Pharisees in everyday life. Then, I introduce a different kind of modern-day Pharisee that I've faced. They don't all look alike—and we will encounter all kinds of Pharisees. But we need to recognize them so we don't become one of them or lose our courage when we face them. Finally, each chapter contains a challenge—some questions to think about—as you follow Jesus into the adventure that He has planned for you.

Whether you go through the questions individually or as part of a group study, they are here to help you delve deeper into your relationship with Him.

Remember, following Jesus is not the easiest path, but it is the best. It is not the safest, but it is His perfect plan. It is a path that is beyond your strength. It is made possible only with the supernatural power of Jesus. All the way along the journey, you will see that He has helped you do more than you could imagine. The adventure in leadership God calls us to is everything we could hope for. But we need to watch out for bears.

QUESTIONS TO THINK ABOUT

1. What are you most afraid Jesus will make you confront?

2. What would keep you from following His path?

3. Have you ever allowed your fear of a Pharisee in your life to stop you from doing something?

4. Do you believe Jesus has a path for you?

5. What Pharisee in your life right now has you afraid?

One

Confront Your Pharisees
or Lose Your Way

We hear branches breaking and the sound of footsteps—something is coming. Our hearts are racing. Our rifles are raised. We can't see what's coming through the thick brush. We think about retreating, but that would put us into even thicker brush. Could we stop a bear in less than fifteen feet after it breaks out of the bushes and trees? Would we be another statistic in grizzly-bear folklore? Are my friends more accurate at shooting than I am? Are they shaking, too? Are their stomachs turning like mine? Are they covered in cold sweat? Is this the beginning of the end?

TIME TO MAN UP

Jim, Paul, and I headed to Alaska in early September of 2003. For years, I had read about Alaskan adventures: moose hunting from rafts, caribou hunting on the tundra, and hiking through the wilderness of Alaska with grizzly bears around every corner. The thought of a dangerous adventure gets the adrenaline flowing in my soul. So I researched and booked a trip out of Anchorage on an air taxi. I began to look for willing participants. I was having a bit of a struggle finding guys to go with me—not everyone trusts me in the woods. My friend Steve says I react well in dangerous situations, but it is usually my fault for getting in them. Over the years, I think I've lost some adventure partners because of some of those dangerous situations. We would get home just fine, but they never wanted to go on another trip with me.

I invited all my regular hunting buddies, but only Paul and Jim agreed to go. I guess I've discovered that they are as crazy as I am. At our first meeting to plan the trip, I pulled out maps of the Mulchatna River drainage in Alaska and all the air-taxi information I'd gathered. It was becoming real to us as we tried to anticipate what to take and what we needed to buy. We shared the books we bought to get ready for the trip—books on how to call a moose, how to judge a caribou and a do-it-yourself hunting book with lists of all we needed to bring. We started to develop our own lists of all we'd need to make this trip happen. I announced to the group that we had a big problem: our plane had a gear weight limit of 125 pounds per person. Our tents, tarps, food, and hunting gear already exceeded that weight limit. We talked about the problem and tossed around some solutions. Finally, I suggested we leave some of our food behind in favor of important gear. We would live off the game we killed. If unsuccessful harvesting a caribou or a moose, we would just be very hungry waiting for the plane to return. Our air-taxi service would drop us off three hours away from the nearest civilization.

The day of our trip finally arrived. My wife, Audrey, dropped us off at Sea-Tac Airport so we could catch our plane. It felt a little funny walking into the airport with a gun case. I was surprised at how easy and safe it was to travel with a gun. Our cases were inspected, locked up, and loaded on the plane. We were on our way. On the plane from Seattle to Anchorage, I pulled out *Mark of the Grizzly*, a book given to me by a friend. This book contains gruesome details about all the bear attacks that have been documented. I read out loud.

As my friends listened, I could see terror spread across their faces. I also felt some fear building in my own gut.

In Anchorage, we transferred our gear from the 737 to a small floatplane, called a Beaver. We finally landed on a small pond in the wilderness. As we got off the plane, the pilot dumped our gear on the ground and said, "There are several campsites somewhere up there in the woods. Good luck." I handed him a one-hundred-dollar bill and said, "Don't forget where we are." He got into his plane and took off. I watched the plane disappear into the sky.

We were alone in the vast wilderness of Alaska. The book of stories had put our senses on high alert. We were convinced that there were grizzlies around every corner, ready to attack.

The view of the Alaska wilderness—looking at our camp by the water.

It was starting to rain, so we lugged our gear up the hill and started setting up camp. We believed that the grizzly bears would be coming by, and we wanted to be ready. We hung the small supply of food we'd brought. We decided to go for a hike and get a feel for the lay of the land. In Alaska, you're not allowed to hunt until the morning after you arrive, so we were just scouting, but we had our rifles to protect us from bears. We were hiking close together for protection.

We made our way about three miles through swamps and thick brush. It was hard going, trudging through brush that

Paul at camp drying wet clothes after a hike.

didn't allow us to see more than a few feet in front of us. We came to a knoll, and the brush began to move. With the attack stories fresh on our minds, we could only fear the worst. We raised our rifles and prepared for the attack. I was so scared, but I felt so alive! I live for the moments when all the senses are on full alert and your fear of death has made your body respond by filling your veins with adrenaline. With rifles raised, the noise got louder. It would break through the brush

Paul (left) and Jim hiking to camp through the thick brush.

about fifteen feet in front of us. We knew it was a grizzly, but we didn't know how it would react or how *we* would react. The fear made me want to run, but I stood still. I could hear my heartbeat, and I felt every breath! Finally, it was so close it was going to break through the final bit of brush.

She stepped out of the bushes, and we were ready to shoot! It was indeed a mother, but not a bear. A forty-year-old mother from Anchorage was bear hunting by herself. She was not a bit worried about the dangers of grizzly bears in the Alaskan wilderness. She didn't even seem alarmed by our rifles. Our fears had gotten the best of us. That day, I learned it was time to face my fears and "man up."

To be truthful, most followers of Jesus have lost their nerve. I think it is time for us to man up and face our fears.

Following Jesus is a dangerous adventure in leadership, but He calls us to it. We want it to be easy and safe. When He walked by those disciples fishing that day, I wonder what they thought they were getting into? To follow Jesus is amazing. His supernatural power works; all we have to do is look at the miracles. His message changes people. Just look at the woman at the well or the woman caught in adultery. He really is the answer this world is looking for. But do I have the courage to follow Him? I started following Christ as a twelve-year-old boy. To be honest, my fear has kept me from following Him at times. But whenever I have the courage to follow Him into the unknown, I am not disappointed. When I follow Him closely, I have to confront the danger of the Pharisees. They come in all shapes and sizes. But I have learned that, to follow Jesus, I have to confront my Pharisees or lose my way.

WHO WERE THE PHARISEES?

Two thousand years ago, Jesus taught His disciples to man up and confront their fears of some powerful people called the Pharisees. As a follower of Jesus, it meant that you would be in a dangerous conflict with the Pharisees. In fact, if you would remove all the conflicts with the Pharisees from the first four books of the New Testament (the ones that detail the life of Christ), you would have almost nothing left. Jesus led His disciples on a path that involved constant conflict with the Pharisees. So who were these men?

The Pharisees of Jesus's time were people of power. The calling of a Pharisee was a great calling. The word Pharisee means "to be separated." They actually started to combat a culture that was moving away from the worship of God, not unlike our culture today. They were bold and fearless as they confronted their dangerous traditions. They opposed a group called the Sadducees. The Sadducees were the wealthy men, born into power by family ties that could be traced all the way to Aaron, Moses's brother. They didn't believe in an afterlife. They believed that if you worshiped at the temple and sacrificed as prescribed, God would bless you and give you a good life on earth. They were not popular with the people. So out of a middle class rose a group of men set apart to do good. It worked! The Pharisees became leaders who ensured that some godly men would stand against the culture and honor God. They were true leaders of their day. They really made a difference.

The Pharisees were chosen by the people and not from a bloodline like the priests. As leaders, they would rise from the crowd and stand up to culture to lead anyone who would follow in a godly direction. They lived their lives differently. They followed all the laws. Their law came from the Torah (the first five books of the Bible) and the oral law from their rabbis, meant to clarify the written law. They followed this law and made sure others did the same. These Pharisees encouraged the worship of God in all the communities. Because of them, there were 480 synagogues and countless schools to worship God. They stood out in the community. Today, the modern synagogue is a result of their movement.

The Pharisees dressed differently, trimmed their hair and beards, and wore long robes and vestiges, which had spiritual meaning. They lived differently; they gave 30 to 40 percent of their income, following the laws of sacrifices and offerings. They memorized the Torah. They followed a daily ritual of prayer; they would stop whatever they were doing to say their prayers three times a day, always facing the temple.

They had a different attitude; they believed they were more righteous and pure than everyone else because they knew more and did more. They were separated holy men of God, so they didn't touch regular people because they might touch someone who was not pure. Any person might contaminate them. They were leaders and expected to be at the front of the line—they hated the back of the line. They expected all to listen and follow as they directed. They had power, and they knew it. Pharisees were good people who had just lost perspective. To them, life had become a list of rules and duties; life was more about what you couldn't do and not about the adventure of becoming something greater.

In order for the disciples of Jesus to discover who they were—and to become who they needed to be—they would have to overcome their fears and face the power of the Pharisees. They would be encountering a Pharisee at every corner, in every community. They would be facing their fears.

FIRST CONFRONTATION WITH THE PHARISEES

Right after selecting His twelve disciples, Jesus sat them down on a mountainside to teach them. This lesson is called the Sermon on the Mount and is the most famous of all His messages. It would be repeated in every community. That is why we have it word for word. It would become the new standard to live by. Jesus placed His disciples right in front of Him for the first teaching of this famous message, but right behind them would have been the Pharisees. They were there to ensure the quality of the teaching. They would have already been miffed that Jesus had not selected His disciples from one of their schools or that Jesus himself had not attended one of their schools. This was not the traditional way to become a rabbi. You could become a rabbi as a Pharisee, but most rabbis were Pharisees first. Jesus was already treading on dangerous ground when He said this:

But I warn you, unless your righteousness surpasses the righteousness of the teachers of religious law and there the Pharisees, you will never enter the Kingdom of Heaven! (Matthew 5:20)

Did Jesus know they were right there? Was He trying to agitate them? This would awaken the mother bear inside the Pharisees. He was teaching His disciples to set their sights higher than those who stood right behind them. I wonder if they could feel that tension? He then went on to set a new standard.

You have heard that our ancestors were told, "You must not murder. If you commit murder, you are subject to judgment." But I say, if you are even angry with someone [without cause], you are subject to judgment. (Matthew 5:21–22)

My guess is that the disciples were already angry with each other. The tax collector Matthew and Simon the zealot would have gone at it. The two sets of fishermen brothers who were in competition on the water were now in competition on the shore. Jesus had just called His disciples murderers. More important, He set an impossible standard for the Pharisees listening in and standing right there.

If you call someone an idiot, you are in danger of being brought before the court. And if you curse someone, you are in danger of the fires of hell. (Matthew. 5:22)

Are you kidding? A curse sends you to hell? Impossible! How are we going to survive on this path?

You have heard the commandment that says, "You must not commit adultery." But I say, anyone who even looks at a woman with lust has already committed adultery with her in his heart. (Matthew 5:27–28)

Jesus just made His disciples adulterers. The standards He was setting were unbelievable. The jaws on those Pharisees must have dropped. The next time you read chapters five through seven of Matthew, read them with the idea of the Pharisees standing behind the disciples. Every word was aimed at them. Jesus taught that one should turn the other cheek, pray in private, pray humbly, forgive quickly, love one's enemies, give quietly, and a host of other teachings that were the opposite of the Pharisees' teachings. At the end of His message, Jesus drew a line in the sand by saying that His message was building on a rock and any other message was shifting sand.

In that first encounter with the Pharisees, Jesus put them on the defensive. He charged them when they least expected it. Jesus didn't pick a fight with the unbelievers or the ungodly. He didn't pick a fight with the Sadducees, who were the wealthy ruling class. He picked a fight with the people who should have been his allies.

The confrontations would come for the next three years. Jesus was leading His disciples into a collision with the most powerful leaders of His day. The Pharisees would see Him as a threat to the traditions they preserved. They would do anything to keep him from changing their world.

The most interesting moments in Jesus's ministry occurred when He confronted the Pharisees. Almost every significant thing that Jesus did happened because of them.

The Pharisees' opposition to Jesus eventually killed Him. But His death created the change that these Pharisees so opposed. His Resurrection changed the disciples and gave them power to face their fears, become leaders, and live the impossible life.

This is the leadership adventure that God is calling us to. The adventure is impossible because it is beyond us and we will have many Pharisees to confront. His spirit is what we need to transform us and give us strength for the impossible adventure—and the power to confront our modern-day Pharisees.

MY DINNER CONVERSATION WITH A PHARISEE

On my leadership adventure, I have run into some Pharisees. For me to follow Jesus means I must be willing to man up and face my fear—even if it costs everything.

God called me into the adventure of ministry at age twelve. I never wavered from wanting that adventure. I went to Bible school, started as a youth minister at age nineteen, and then at age twenty-five, I led my first church in Monterey, California. God helped me in those early days in ways I never dreamed possible. It is amazing what happens when you let God lead you. We grew from a church of forty to three hundred people in just three years. I loved those people, and they loved me. I was seeing God's hand at work as people came to Christ almost every week. Our little church in Monterey was such a great place, and God did some incredible things.

After three years, I really felt God leading me to a new adventure. I was asked to consider following a pastor who had been at his church for thirty-three years. He had not changed much in all those years; he had been there so long that when they moved his desk, the carpet under it was a different color. But they had just built a big new building, and I thought that, after our success in Monterey, this would be an exciting opportunity to fill that building. Many told me that it was not a good idea to follow a guy who had been in a church for so many years. This was not my leadership adventure, though, and I was doing my best to listen to God.

So I interviewed to become pastor in Concord, California. On the night of the interview, I met Charlie. I had heard about him and was told to watch out for him. He was on the church board that would hire me, and he was a volunteer staff worship leader that would work for me. He was generous with his money and time. He was trying to live right, and he was undoubtedly committed. I liked Charlie; he seemed harmless. But I would soon come to realize that Charlie was a modern-day Pharisee. He was dangerously powerful.

Charlie invited my wife, Audrey, and me to dinner. We ordered expensive steaks. He was paying for this meal to get to know me. He had heard a lot about the growth at our church and had some concerns. It did not take long for me to discover the reason we were there; he was concerned about my strength of leadership. The last pastor had let Charlie lead from behind the scenes for the past few years. Charlie liked his routine, but it was one of the reasons the church was not growing.

Would I challenge his power? Would I be his friend or foe? Would I allow him to continue as he had for the last twenty years with his choir and style of music? He was in charge, and it was evident that he did not want anyone meddling with his traditions. I soon realized that he was stuck in a rut, unable to change. His style of music had become his god; it was destroying him and his church. If I were to challenge him, it was going to be dangerous.

Would I be brave enough to confront this well-meaning Pharisee? Or would I just allow him to lead me? Would I take the safe route or face my Pharisee?

Everyone has to face his or her Pharisees. They are in businesses, churches, governments, and even in families. To confront them means they will attack. Am I willing to live an adventure that leads to change and life? If I didn't confront this Pharisee, I would lose my way. I am convinced many people lose their way because they are afraid of their Pharisee.

I explained to Charlie the adventurous path that Christ was leading me on. I talked to him about how people were finding Christ in our ministry. I couldn't wait to see what God would do at this church. I was committed to change whatever needed to be changed to help us reach the lost. I needed Charlie to hear my heart and hoped he, too, would hear the heart of God. I wanted him to embrace a change that would bring him life—and life to the church he loved.

"I am the music pastor. Hymns are the only type of music that have real depth. Too many people are abandoning music that matters," Charlie said.

I was taken aback by his answer. Was he listening? Did he hear the words I was saying? I hadn't really said anything about music.

"What if the best way to reach people involves a different style of music?" I asked.

"We sing hymns; this is what the church likes. This is the music *I* like," he replied.

Still, he was not listening. He was adamant about his agenda. His heart was not open to change or to my leadership. I was not getting through to him. This was a sad moment—I realized he cared more about music style than about the people God wanted us to reach. Did he care about the lost soul?

"Charlie, if I become the pastor and you are the music leader, we will do whatever it takes to reach the lost," I said.

"Hymns *do* reach the lost. They have for years. If hymns have worked in the past, then they will work today," he replied.

It was clear—he had now played his cards. What I would do next would define the future of my ministry. I had to man up and confront my fear and face my Pharisee.

"This is no longer about hymns and music; this is about leadership," I replied. This is the adventure God has called me to. Here is the real question: if I become pastor, will you follow me? Charlie, when I become pastor, we will select music that will best reach the culture we live in. Some of it you will like, and some of it you won't. Are you okay with that?"

It was essential to find out if this person, who was a powerful, highly respected man, would let me lead him out of his Pharisee mentality. Could he listen and follow and make the change?

"As long as it's music that we like!" Charlie answered (he would not give up his rights).

Speaking confidently—and preparing Charlie for the idea that I'd get the job—I said, "Be ready. On the first Sunday, we will do music that is not your kind of music. Are you going to be all right with that? If you are not all right with it, I can't have you work for me." My job sometimes calls me to fire volunteers. This is not an easy task.

It was evident that the expensive steak was turning in his stomach. Dinner's agenda had changed. His anxiety was increasing to the point that his face turned flush, looking as if it were going to explode. I felt sorry for him; his anger toward me would escalate. He was out of control. Confronting a Pharisee is not easy.

He left the dinner table abruptly and never answered my question. He reluctantly paid the bill and left in a hurry. Audrey was upset with me. She did not understand what was happening. She had no idea this would be a defining moment in our ministry. Why was I so hard on him, on someone I just met? Why did I push him so hard? Audrey is a much nicer person than I am; I knew I had to do this. When you confront your Pharisees, even those closest to you often misunderstand your actions and intent. I also knew this would not be the last time I would hear from Charlie—he was a Pharisee, and he would use his power.

Charlie went back to meet with the board. He met privately and publicly with many people to influence them against me. He ultimately cast his vote against me at the board meeting. Despite his influence, miraculously, the board allowed my name to be presented to the congregation for a congregational vote.

Before that Sunday, Charlie wielded his power to try to influence as many as possible to vote against me. A little over one hundred people voted that day. One-quarter of them voted against me. This was considered a terrible vote. But I looked at it as a miracle. I won by one percentage point. I had already decided that I would let God help me with this impossible adventure, no matter what the Pharisee did.

We had some great days at that church. They were hard days, filled with confrontations with various Pharisees, but God's work always breaks through when we let it. I went to Charlie's house before he left the church to meet one last time. His wife told me I had put her into menopause early. I laugh out loud thinking about this Pharisee. And I cry inside, hoping that he will find real life through a leadership adventure with Christ.

QUESTIONS TO THINK ABOUT

1. Who are you in these stories? The crowd? The committed? A Pharisee?

2. Are you on the edge of deciding to follow Jesus on your adventure?

3. What are you afraid of?

4. Are you confronted with a Pharisee who has you in his/her eyes of judgment?

5. What will you do? What should you do?

6. Are you a Pharisee? Be honest.

7. Are you a good person caught up in a tradition that has lost its power?

8. Do you believe that Jesus loves you?

9. What do you need to do to join His adventure?

TWO

Looking at the Pharisee in Me

The video recorder time stamp says 1:59 p.m. It is October 5, 2003. Because the lens cap is on, there is no video, just audio. Investigators believe that Timothy and Amie have gone into the tent to eat a little lunch and get out of the rain. Tim then steps outside. It becomes evident that a bear has entered their camp.

Soon Amie is heard saying "Is it still out there?"

Timothy screams, "Get out here! I'm getting killed out here!" There are sounds of rain and wind on the tent and sounds of Timothy fighting to "Play dead!" Amie yells again, "Play dead!"

The bear breaks off the attack. Amie and Tim try to determine if the bear is really gone. The bear returns to attack Timothy. Timothy cries out "playing dead isn't working" and begs her to "hit the bear!"

The wind and the rain from the storm are clearly heard, then Amie yells "Fight back!" She is screaming, "Stop! Go away!" or possibly, "Run Away!" A sound of a frying pan striking the bear is heard.

Amie begins screaming very loudly, as Tim is saying "Amie get away, get away, go away I am dying."

Amie did not go away.

There are sounds of the bear dragging Timothy off and the fading sounds of his screams. Tim is being pulled and dragged into the brush and away from camp.

Amie begins a high-pitched scream that sounds much like an animal in distress. The investigators believe this is the reason the bear returns some time after that to kill Amie.

(All quotes from the videotape come from the investigators, Alaska State biologist, Larry Van Daele, 2004, medical examiner, and Franc Fallico, 2004. To date, they are the only ones who have listened to the tape.)

PROTECTION THAT WENT TOO FAR

That horrific encounter was of Timothy Treadwell and his girlfriend, Amie Huguenard, during their last moments of life. This attack is rare (there have been only five hundred since the year 1900), and even more rare is the return of the bear for a second fatal attack. For thirteen years, Timothy traveled to Katmai National Park and stayed at a place he called the Grizzly Maze. It was Timothy's belief system that took them to the place where they eventually ended up getting killed.

Timothy believed that he was a protector of bears, even though they were protected in Katmai National Park. He dedicated his summers to travel to defend them from poaching, even though there was no evidence that poaching had ever occurred.

He believed these were *his* bears and that he understood them and they understood him. He was convinced that the rules of dealing with grizzly bears did not apply to him. His system of beliefs was so embedded in his mind that he disregarded normal precautions, such as portable electric fences, lethal force, and pepper sprays. He believed he was different from everyone else.

Timothy also convinced others to think as he did, regardless of the real dangers that were involved. He persuaded his girlfriend, Amie, to join him on that year's expedition. She was never comfortable with the bears. In her journal, she even expressed fears and longed for the day when they would return home. She was only one day away from going home. The plane would come to pick them up the very next day at 2 p.m. and discover the remains of Timothy and Amie.

For thirteen years, he acted as the protector of bears who were already protected in Katmai National Park. Every year, Timothy left Kodiak Island, where the bears are hunted legally and are *not* protected. The bears on Kodiak Island are managed, and harvest tags are issued every year. The population is stable and well controlled and grosses four and a half million dollars a year in income for this community. Kodiak is also a place where one has to be exceptionally cautious because the Kodiak bears are more aggressive than those in Katmai. Timothy would not be able to live amongst the bears on Kodiak as he did in Katmai.

Timothy's hypocritical stance of "saving the grizzlies" fueled many debates in the local Kodiak city bars, especially when he passed through. If Timothy truly believed he was meant to protect bears, he could have stayed at Kodiak Island where they were hunted, but he didn't. Instead, he traveled to Katmai to protect bears that were *already* protected.

It appeared that almost everything in Timothy's life was a lie. He said he was an orphan from England, when his parents actually lived in Long Island, New York. His true identity was Timothy Dexter, not Treadwell. He was not the person he claimed to be. He said he protected bears, but his death initiated the first killing of any bear in the eight-five-year history of Katmai National Park. When five park rangers arrived to recover the bodies of Timothy and Amie and to investigate the surroundings, a large grizzly charged them at less than twenty feet. After fifteen shots, the bear died twelve feet away. The remains of Timothy were found inside the bear. Another bear charged rangers while they were loading the remains of Timothy and Amie onto the helicopter. Warning shots were fired, but the bear kept coming and had to be killed. The larger bear was tagged and well known to the rangers, but the second bear was a smaller bear and not yet tagged. Timothy would also be responsible for the killing of his latest girlfriend, Amie.

Timothy believed that because the bears understood him, they would never attack him. However, in 2003, the salmon count was lower than normal, and the bears were hungrier than normal—and they attacked. That year, he stayed at the park one week longer than his usual stay. It ended up being one day too long: the bears were starving. Unfortunately, Timothy became their meal. The floatplane pilot that showed up that day to pick up Timothy and Amie found the bear eating them. He flew over fifteen times in an attempt to get the bear to move away. The bear only ate faster. Timothy Treadwell was the first human fatality from a grizzly bear in the park's eighty-five year history.

During his lifetime, Timothy appeared on late-night shows preaching his beliefs. He had an appearance on *Dateline* and the Discovery Channel. He traveled to every school that would have him, encouraging his philosophy. He raised thousands of dollars to support his beliefs. I think he truly loved grizzly bears. But he needed them more than they needed him. And although he was a sincere person, he was committed to a hypocritical and dangerous belief system.

Today, a group called *Grizzly People* carries on Timothy's teachings and views. An ex-girlfriend named Jewel runs the organization, and you can still donate to support Timothy's beliefs. His films are still shown, and the hypocrisy of his beliefs has never been admitted. One day, it will kill another it is meant to protect.

While is easy for me to see the Pharisee in Timothy, can I see the Pharisee in myself? On our leadership adventure, Jesus has a way of exposing the Pharisee in me.

JESUS EXPOSES THE PHARISEE:
WHO THROWS THE FIRST STONE?

But early the next morning He was back again at the Temple. A crowd soon gathered, and He sat down and taught them. As He was speaking, the teachers of religious law and the Pharisees brought a woman who had been caught in the act of adultery. They put her in front of the crowd. (John 8:2-3)

The Pharisees confronted Jesus with a woman "caught in the very act of adultery." She was probably naked (they may have wrapped a sheet around her). We don't really know. What I do know is that these Pharisees did not care how they embarrassed this woman. I have to ask, "Why didn't they bring the man?" How did they know where to find this woman in the very act? I'm confident the Pharisees were not pure in their thinking. They had just watched and interrupted a sex act. They were filled with lust, the same as any other man. Their minds were not pure; this was an ancient form of pornography. I wonder if they had done this before.

The Pharisees took the naked woman (we don't even know her name) and dragged her around the city of Jerusalem looking for Jesus. They thought Jesus was too soft on sin. He was too kind to sinners. They thought He was too quick to forgive. His ranks were full of sinners like this and Mary Magdalene, who was known for her terrible past. It seemed as if every disciple who followed Jesus was a sinner. The Pharisees would not have allowed His followers to touch them; it would have soiled their purity. They were certain that Jesus would ignore a well-known law on adultery and forgive. I wonder if they had listened to the Sermon on the Mount when Jesus declared that adultery begins with a look of lust. They sought to expose Him, but were they ready to be exposed? This is a defining moment in Jesus's ministry. The sin of this woman was obvious to all. What would He do?

They were trying to trap Him into saying something they could use against Him, but Jesus stooped down and wrote in the dust with His finger. (John 8:6)

Jesus drew in the sand. There is a lot of speculation on why He did this. These are my thoughts: I believe He chose to divert His eyes away so that His earthly body would not respond to the exposed woman. I think we need to remember that although Jesus was the Son of God, He was also a human man.

They kept demanding an answer, so He stood up again and said, "All right, but let the one who has never sinned throw the first stone!" Then He stooped down again and wrote in the dust. When the accusers heard this, they slipped away one by one, beginning with the oldest, until only Jesus was left in the middle of the crowd with the woman. (John 8:7-9)

With his head looking down, Jesus had agreed that the woman had committed adultery. She deserved to die by stoning because of her sin. Think about it: He agreed with them. This is hard for us because we live in a world that doesn't like to call sin, sin. Jesus said to them, "Whoever has never sinned throw the first stone." Then, from the oldest to youngest, they left. I think they felt guilty because of their own lust that day. Their sins were standing in front of them—their sins were lust and pornography.

Jesus was left alone with the naked woman. He was the only man that never sinned who could actually throw the first stone, but He didn't. He gave her an opportunity to change. He gave her a fresh start. He told her to "go and sin no more."

This is a story of the Pharisees catching a sinner and bringing her to Jesus. Jesus, having an opportunity to show grace, forgave her. He gave her a new beginning after exposing the Pharisees' sin. I hope the woman changed. I hope the Pharisees changed. Most of all, I hope I have changed by facing the Pharisee exposed in me.

DISCOVERING THE PHARISEE IN ME

I meet Pharisees all the time. They are easy to recognize and confront. When confronted, they make defining moments in my ministry. I can see them clearly because I have discovered the Pharisee in myself.

At age thirty-three, I died because of my beliefs. My dangerous traditions killed me. I was in a church that talked about living above sin, and yet I was sinning. I preached about family and its importance, but I was neglecting my own because I had become absorbed with helping others. I preached about balance, but I was addicted to success and the work that was produced and did not practice balance. I was living hypocritical beliefs, and they killed me.

So, what were my beliefs? I believed my sole responsibility in life was to save the marriages—and the families—of others. I would drop everything to counsel, nurture, and encourage, and I was exceptionally proficient at it. I spent all my creative energy on everyone else's relationships but my own. In the middle of dinner, I always took a phone call. If a family called having trouble with their kids while I was playing with my own, I took the call. Too often, my wife would see me choose ministry over her. My kids would see me choose others over them.

By the time I would arrive home to my wife, my creativity and energy were spent. I did not reserve for her what she deserved. My kids needed to know they mattered, but my actions showed them differently. I helped every other family's children but didn't take the time and effort to help my own. My dangerous traditions were destroying me; it was evident that my soul needed to be nourished.

Deep in my heart, I believed if I worked for God I would be valuable. I did work hard on a daily basis and felt respected. The work I did was beneficial to everyone except the ones who truly mattered. I wanted my family to value me, but I was of no value to them. They needed me to turn my heart toward them so we could thrive. I had to learn that God valued me because He loved me, not because of what I did.

One day, my world changed. I was confronted with my own sins. My life was full of excess. I worked especially long hours during the week, striving for success. I filled my life with everything but God while constantly trying to work for Him. One night after a twenty-hour day, I was taken to the hospital after losing all my fluids by throwing up, having diarrhea, and experiencing severe sweats. When the medics arrived, they could not find a pulse. They thought I had had a heart attack.

I soon discovered that I had Ménière's disease, which deprived me of hearing in my right ear and gave me dizzy spells that would make the world spin. I endured attacks every three days that made it impossible to keep up with the pace I was living. While the attacks were not enough to keep me from my responsibilities as pastor, the disease revealed my hypocrisy. I began to examine my life. My health made me realize that there were many areas of hypocrisy in me. I made a decision to live differently.

It was then that I decided to take a year off work so I could restore my health. In April, I attended an Easter service, and for the first time, I was not preaching. I remember thinking,

This is the year that I died. I asked the Lord to please resurrect me for His glory, and He did.

I used that sabbatical year to restore my soul and my family. It was the best decision I ever made. I spent all my time loving my family and rebuilding my marriage. Audrey and I did some counseling to strengthen our relationship. I did some personal counseling to learn why I had lost my way. I began discovering God's love for me and realized I was valuable even when I was not working for Him.

Still, that year was not easy. I lost my wealth. All the money I had saved was gone, and the rest was taken in a failed real-estate deal. It was at that point that my health got worse. I had become bedridden every three days from the attacks of Ménière's disease. Nonetheless, my soul was restored, and my marriage and family were renewed. I never again want to return to that hypocritical belief system.

My heart goes out to all Pharisees. It is impossible to be the perfect judge. It will not end well for them. Their only hope for attaining life is the death and resurrection of their souls. Like Jesus, I want to expose their hypocrisy, not to be cruel but to help them discover a different way to believe and live.

QUESTIONS TO THINK ABOUT

1. What people are you most judgmental of? Why?

2. Is there someone in your life who has become untouchable because you think he or she is a sinner?

3. What person would you drag in front of Jesus to be judged?

4. Who is the Pharisee in you?

5. Have you ever felt like that woman embarrassed by her sin?

6. Can you pray and ask God to forgive the Pharisee in you?

Three

The Pharisee
Has Changed

When I look up, the six-hundred-pound grizzly bear is running right toward us. He's a couple of hundred yards away. With every stride, he effortlessly eats up the distance between us. He's trotting at a fast pace. He doesn't seem to be charging, but he will soon notice us—and then what? My heart races as I stand there with only a fishing rod—I'm counting on the others to protect me with their rifles. I spin around to see where my companions are. I'm shocked. I'm alone. They've retreated to higher ground!

EQUIPPED WITH A FISHING ROD

On this particular trip, I chose to go caribou hunting. My son, Daniel, son-in-law, Brian, and a close friend Chet made up our hunting party. We boarded a 737 in Seattle with all our gear and headed to our destination, Prudhoe Bay/ Deadhorse, Alaska, which is located way above the Arctic Circle. This was my third trip caribou hunting in Alaska and their very first. I wanted them to experience Alaska's backcountry as I had. Adventure changes you and shapes your future. I wanted them to experience the wild and to enjoy an adventure of a lifetime.

Once again, as I did on my first trip to Alaska, I read aloud from the book, *Mark of the Grizzly*. With explicit detail, it describes terrifying grizzly bear attacks that have occurred during the last century. One attack that I read described how a couple was stalked by a grizzly that followed them—even after they attempted to avoid him by moving away. The bear eventually caught them and attacked the man. His wife beat on the bear until it turned and attacked her. The man went for help only to come back and find that the bear had devoured his wife. My intent was to get my companions' blood pumping and to raise fears—and I did! Looks of anxiety spread across their faces as we read the gory details of that story and others.

They all knew they would have to face their fears, venture outside their comfort zones, and take risks. Adventure is all about the unknown. Something inside all of us draws us to adventure. The fear that comes from the unknown has *always* made me feel alive. Fear makes you stay in the moment. You have to live in the now, confronting your fear head-on and engaging it. It gives me a rush of adrenaline that I am addicted to.

On arrival in Alaska, an air-taxi service picked us up for the two-hour drive to a remote gravel runway where we would board a two-person Super Cub. We'd then fly approximately two hours into the wilderness to be dropped off and left alone on the Alaskan tundra.

The Super Cub limited us to seventy-five pounds for each person, and that included our rifles. Because of the weight limit, we had to be practical about what we brought. We chose to leave some food behind to make room for needed gear. This was a risky strategy, but it was our hope that we would be successful when hunting; it would be our only means to supplement the little food we brought for our seven-day stay in Alaska.

The scenery from the plane was spectacular! We saw caribou, grizzly bears, and the beautiful countryside. After the two-hour plane ride at about one-thousand-feet elevation, we landed on a flat spot in the middle of nowhere. After finding a campsite, we set up our tents. As Chet set his up, he was sure to keep someone else in-between him and where he thought a bear might come from. Clearly, the bear stories were on his mind. There were lots of grizzly bears in this area; we had seen three on the way in. We all knew a bear encounter was inevitable; we were just waiting for that moment.

The first few days, we did see a number of grizzlies about a mile or two away. We were thankful they kept their distance.

From left: My son, Daniel; son-in-law, Brian; and me during our successful caribou-hunting trip.

Our trip was successful beyond our wildest dreams. We harvested five caribou near our camp. We carried the meat to the campsite in our backpacks so we could transport it back home. The caribou season was in full swing, and we were allowed two each. Our meat was stored one hundred yards from the campsite in case a bear wanted to eat from it.

We were always alert looking for bears. We were also always looking toward the cache of meat to make sure there were no bears. We knew that grizzlies in that area were already putting on weight for the long winter hibernation ahead.

Grizzlies can sometimes eat twelve hours a day. If they found a hoard of meat, there would be some serious problems. We would lose a portion of our meat and would have to scare them away so we could relocate our camp and our meat. Most of the time, grizzlies run from people. They have a God-given natural fear of man. But when they claim a food cache, it can turn into a dangerous and deadly situation. They become defensive of "their" food and get much more aggressive. Many bear attacks come when a person stumbles onto a bear's food cache and the animal assumes the human is a thief and needs to be punished for stealing the goods.

Since our hunt for caribou was so successful, all we had left to do was wait for the air taxi to come pick us up. With two days to kill, I suggested we attempt the two-mile hike across the tundra to fish at a creek we'd seen upon landing. I chose to bring *only* my fishing rod since the other three were carrying their rifles. I decided to rely on them and their firepower to protect me if we encountered a grizzly bear. We all knew to be exceptionally cautious. Since the grizzlies north of the Arctic Circle rarely see humans, they can be extremely aggressive. Grizzlies there can live their whole lives without seeing a single person, and since they are on top of the food chain, anything is fair game.

While hiking into the valley, we wandered around a bend, and there he was! The grizzly was two hundred yards away and on the side of a hill, trotting right toward us. I immediately said to everyone, "Stand your ground!" I told them not to run because you cannot outrun a bear. There were two things we needed to do: be ready to make some noise and look larger than we actually were. A bear is more likely to leave if confronted by something he perceives to be more intimidating. I knew this was a dangerous situation. He hadn't noticed us yet, and we outnumbered him, so stopping him from charging would be a lot easier. However, without a rifle, all I could do was make my stand with my fishing rod in hand. I decided since I didn't have a rifle I would videotape the bear. I took out the camera and began to record the encounter.

I knew not to look at him straight in the eye; such a challenge could make him attack. But I did look in his direction. He was amazing. Massive. Muscular. Impressive. We decided to make some noise. We yelled, "Hey bear! Hey bear!" Human yelling often diverts a bear, and it was the only deterrent we had left to stop him in his tracks. I looked back to make sure the others were still together to make us look intimidating. Suddenly, I realized I was alone—all three had retreated to higher ground! I couldn't believe it. I thought we were standing our ground. I hollered, "Where are you guys?"

I nervously scanned the area and saw they had climbed up a hill. I quickly joined them. We yelled, waved, and clapped our hands, but the bear was still coming—by then, it was about one hundred yards away. Things were getting a little tense. I begged everyone to please stand his ground and not run. I desperately needed them to defend me; I did not have a rifle or even bear spray.

We yelled at him again, "Hey bear! Get out of here! Leave us alone!" It finally worked! He suddenly stopped in midstride. He turned around and went back from the direction he had come. With more confidence, we continued to yell as he ran from us.

Although somewhat shaken by the experience, I still wanted to go fishing. "Let's go!" I said. "No way!" the others replied. However, they finally agreed to go if I led the way with my fishing rod, so I did. We hiked downstream in the same paw prints of the grizzly. I led them down the valley, talking loudly to our bear just in case he was in the vicinity.

I had a different attitude on this trip than on my first one. I was becoming familiar with bears. I was learning to relax and enjoy and let the adventure unfold. I knew what to expect and that much of the bears' behavior was out of my control, so I began to truly enjoy the encounters. I had changed. I no longer let my fears control me. I no longer cowered at the thought of facing a grizzly. I knew that the hike was going to be enjoyable, even though we were in grizzly territory. This trip became more than a caribou-hunting trip; it was also an adventure for we had faced our fears.

God isn't interested in a life that has no adventure. When we get to the end of our lives, we should be saying, "Wow!" not, "Is that it?" So many in our world today hurry to get married, raise a family, have a successful career, and then say, "Is that it?" For many, it is enough to kill them. That is why so many die upon retiring.

God wants you to join His leadership adventure. Just as a reminder though, it has bears. Their names are the Pharisees. But the great thing about them is they don't always attack— sometimes they make an about-face.

TWO PHARISEES MAKE AN ABOUT-FACE

Jesus's death brought a surprising change in two Pharisees. John Mark wrote the book of Mark and was from a family that was well placed in the leadership structure of the Pharisees. Mark would have known Joseph of Arimathea.

Joseph of Arimathea took a risk [faced his fears] and went to Pilate, asking for Jesus's body. Joseph was an honored member of the high council, and waiting for the Kingdom of God to come. (Mark 15:43)

John, the Lord's closest disciple, who is the only one who remained at the cross, gave us more details.

Afterwards, Joseph, a secret disciple of Jesus, because he feared the Jewish leaders, asked Pilate for permission to take down Jesus's body. When Pilate consented, he took it. (John 19:38)

For a Pharisee to change, he has to risk it all and let go of his reputation. Joseph took that risk. He no longer feared his peers. He knew his actions would put him in conflict with those who accompanied him in the high council. This was the very group of Pharisees who killed Jesus. This certainly cost him his position, his power, and his reputation.

However, it did not matter any longer. Joseph wanted to do this for Jesus. Joseph was a secret believer. Something Jesus said, or how He lived, changed Joseph, and his secret was out. He would never again be a secret disciple. He would never again be a Pharisee. He was a follower of Jesus and willing to risk his reputation and join the adventure into the unknown. It is essential to understand that nobody can be a secret disciple. He or she must overcome the fear of man. This was that moment for Joseph. Joseph's heart had changed.

Joseph took a dangerous risk. He did not listen to the advice of his friends, the rabbis, or the teachings of other Pharisees. He gave everything up when he took down the body of Jesus. It is difficult to imagine his thoughts at that time. Was it, *It is better late than never* or *I can't be silent anymore*? To make such a serious decision and then follow through with it, you know it required a lot of thought and consideration. His reputation was on the line. He no longer would be respected and hold his place of power.

Nonetheless, Joseph knew he had to do it. When he gave Jesus his tomb, it likely meant that Joseph, too, might actually join Jesus. If the Pharisees had killed one innocent man, what was one more? Joseph gave up his fears for Christ.

So many people live their lives in the shadows. They secretly believe in Jesus's teachings and are followers, but the Pharisees run their lives. They live in fear, never willing to take a risk. This would be a life-changing moment for Joseph, a moment when he gave God all of himself.

God does extraordinary things when you give up your whole self and risk it all. Because of such a risk, Joseph would never be able to return to his old life. I wish I knew what happened after that, but I believe God filled him with His Spirit, thus having his *own* story to tell of the power of God.

With Joseph came Nicodemus, the man who had come to Jesus at night. He brought roughly seventy-five pounds of perfumed ointment made from myrrh and aloes. (John 19:39)

Nicodemus was the Pharisee that sought out Jesus in the night. You can find his story in John 3:

There was a man named Nicodemus, a Jewish religious leader who was a Pharisee. After dark one evening, he came to speak with Jesus. "Rabbi," he said, "we all know that God has sent You to teach us. Your miraculous signs are evidence that God is with You." (John 3:1-2)

Pharisees were leaders. They were well respected. They were not taught—they did the teaching. They were passionately the best, and they knew it. Over the years, pride had crept into their ranks, and it was a big deal to recognize another rabbi. Jesus was a carpenter, not a Pharisee. He didn't go through the accepted method of becoming a rabbi. His chosen disciples were a disgrace to the Pharisees. This secret visit was the beginning of change. It would have shaken the foundations of Nicodemus's fellow Pharisees to call Jesus a rabbi in the daylight. But here he was, ready to learn.

Jesus replied, "I tell you the truth, unless you are born again, you cannot see the Kingdom of God." "What do You mean?" exclaimed Nicodemus. "How can an old man go back into his mother's womb and be born again?" Jesus replied, "I assure you, no one can enter the Kingdom of God without being born of water and the Spirit." (John 3:3–5)

Nicodemus wanted to know how to get right with God, for Jesus's challenges had penetrated his cold heart. Over the years, Nicodemus had become a true Pharisee. The teaching of his rabbi became his path. The rabbi taught him that if he followed thousands of rules and lived a set-apart, perfect life he could make it to Heaven. This eventually hardened his heart. Jesus's words and life would shake him so hard his heart would eventually crack open.

God sent His Son into the world not to judge the world, but to save the world through Him. There is no judgment against anyone who believes in Him. But anyone who does not believe in Him has already been judged for not believing in God's one and only Son. (John 3:17–18)

As a Pharisee, judging the world had been Nicodemus's job. Judging is what he expected from Jesus. Instead, he discovered the love of God. There is nothing more powerful in this world than love. God leads us into our adventure with love. He knows we are messed up. He knows we mess up. He knows our nature, and He knows the only thing that will truly change us is God's love. When I know how much God loves me, it changes me and makes me happy to let Him lead my life.

Jesus's teachings touched and motivated Nicodemus, but it was not until this point that he changed. This time, he no longer came to Jesus at night, hiding his secret because he feared his peers. He now visited Him in the day, and he brought his wealth along with him. He had seventy-five pounds of ointment that would have cost $150,000 to $200,000 in today's economy. Giving changes people—and here we see the change in Nicodemus. He was willing to give whatever he could in honor of the one who had changed his life.

Jesus's life changed Joseph and Nicodemus. His death changed them even more. I think anyone who sincerely looks at the death of Christ is a changed person forever. When Jesus cried from the cross saying, "Forgive them for they do not know what they are doing," He was speaking to Joseph and Nicodemus, and to each of us. By coming forward, Joseph and Nicodemus changed because of Jesus. They were no longer Pharisees. They knew their peers would reject them and their friends would question them, but they were transformed forever.

God used two Pharisees who made an about-face to ensure that the Resurrection of Jesus was recorded in history. Without these two men, we would not have proof of the Resurrection. Their courage gave Jesus a tomb that would be guarded by soldiers and sealed with a Roman government seal—to break that seal would bring death. It provided crucial evidence that Jesus rose from the grave. If it weren't for Joseph and Nicodemus, the soldiers would have taken His body to the local dump and burned it with the garbage. Their changed hearts show that God can use any Pharisee who is willing to follow. Jesus is the only one who can truly change people.

RISKING IT ALL BRINGS CHANGE

I am a changed Pharisee, too. I know what it is like to change. After a year away from ministry, I was ready for a new leadership adventure that involved starting a church. This time, I was not going to allow others to influence my thoughts or decisions. This new direction made me wonder who I would become and how others would define me. Regardless, I had to leave my reputation aside and do something crazy and take a risk, just like Joseph and Nicodemus. I needed to let *God* change my life.

The biggest obstacle I had to overcome was the physical limitation from Ménière's disease that had been controlling my life for the previous two years. Doctors had not discovered the cause of the disease, so they were only able to treat symptoms.

When the Ménière's attacks escalated, the world around me would spin, and I would lose all fluids within a thirty-minute timeframe. I had little warning, and no one could help me. The doctors provided treatment after treatment for the symptoms, but they didn't work. I eventually learned that the disease would not kill me; it just tortured me for a few hours every other day.

During those moments, I understood what it felt like to wish for the relief of death. This disease made me helpless. It taught me how fragile life is and how we often take our health for granted. The question remained, *How could I be of any value to God?*

I believe the disease was like the Pharisee within me. However, God was helping me change. I took a risk and decided that I would give God all my good days. The days when I was sick, I would just endure the pain. With my wife's blessing, off we went to start a church.

Audrey and I agreed on a little place in Mill Creek, Washington. The night before moving day, my family got together and prayed for my healing. At that point, it did not seem to be working. However, I believed God was still doing a great work in me. His timing is not my timing. Dizzy spells seemed to hit me every three days and would lay me up for one full day. A couple of times, they required trips to the emergency room. My chance to start a church seemed impossible. My ministry and my dream were dead—I needed a resurrection.

On moving day, my wife, two kids, one bird, and a dog crammed into the front cab of a U-Haul, while towing a vehicle behind. As we traveled over Stevens Pass, I had a Ménière's attack. This was a moment of trust for me. I gave God all my worries and then continued driving. When we finally made it to the house rental, I fell on the lawn and lapsed into a full Ménière's attack. I could not help my family unload the truck that day.

Although my pain persisted, I was committed to God and thanked Him for the health that I did have. At that moment, God completed His work in me. I never again had another attack. His healing began from the inside and moved its way out. It would have been impossible for me to continue if God had not intervened. The miracle of healing is often misunderstood. There was no guarantee my health would be restored. There *would* be a miracle though. I believed that God could use a sick man to start a church or heal me to help me in my endeavor. Either one would have taken a miracle of God to achieve.

Risking it all for me changed the person I was. I left behind my reputation, my desire for power, and my influences within my denomination. It was then that I allowed God to take control of everything.

My work to plant a church began by reaching out to all the Christian contacts I had. I challenged them to join me in planting a new church. I eventually had ten couples that were willing to help. I worked round the clock to get them committed. We had meetings as often as they were available. I expressed to them the hard work of planting a church and the challenge this would bring them spiritually.

After a few months, my wife and I invited the couples over for a New Year's gathering. We stretched our budget to the max and bought food for the occasion. We wanted to toast the New Year, pray for God's help, and organize the groundwork. The only problem was nobody showed up. It was obvious they would not be there to help me plant this church. The next morning, I wrote in my journal:

We cried ourselves to sleep. I have failed.
Everything I planned and worked at for three
months is over. I am finished, and so is my
reputation. Everyone is expecting success, but
we are failing. What would I say to investors
that gave to start our church? How could
I live with myself? This is truly one of the
lowest points of my life. What do I do?

Was I not listening? Did I hear wrong? Was my healing for nothing?

On a rainy morning in January, I had to do something. At this point, I had no choice; I did what I did not want to do. I went door-to-door inviting neighbors to a Bible study. I was a depressed man walking in the rain, encouraging people to attend something that I thought would surely fail. I had lost all confidence, but at least I was doing something. It was my way of showing that I was not a quitter. I would keep striving, regardless if I failed.

At each house, I stood with my back to the door and said, "Hey, I know you probably have something else going. I know you probably don't want to come, but I am inviting you to our house for a Bible study." I handed them a flyer and left.

I have to admit, doing this was extremely painful. I only had enough courage to go to twenty houses, ten up one side of the street and ten down the other. I then went home, expecting failure.

It was a Tuesday night. We waited to see if anyone would show. Audrey had the coffee on and a room prepared for children. My mind was set for failure. How in the world could this feeble attempt work? It was downright excruciating! I could not even look out the window—I just stared at the wall and waited. Finally, people arrived. By the end of the night, forty had showed up: twenty adults and twenty children. I know I will never again have such success going door-to-door. Believe me, I've tried. That was a true miracle! I needed that miracle!

Audrey took the twenty kids in the family room, and I had twenty adults in the living room. Our Bible study consisted of a debate with an atheist on the existence of God. However, the miracle of Gold Creek Church came from this little Bible study.

Five couples out of the ten agreed to be my core group— an atheist ("Don't tell anyone that I believe; I'm just doing a good deed socially"), a Jewish couple ("I really don't believe in Jesus, but I want to help you"), a Christian Scientist ("I can help you with the music, but I need it to work around my Christian Science services"), a nominal Christian and her alcoholic husband ("What can I do to help?"), and an Italian Catholic and his evangelical wife ("We will help you for a few months").

This was my core group. We met weekly for three months planning the new church. Believe me, this did *not* help my reputation. The language and behavior of the core group did not meet the expectations of most Christians, but I was desperate. I tried to do everything within my power to accomplish the impossible. However, it was not my call—God chose those people to help build the church. The risk became a true miracle! Because God used those five couples, we have Gold Creek today.

Through the health crisis and the starting of the new church, I learned about taking a risk and trusting God. I wonder what it was like for Joseph to enter the tomb and lay Jesus's body down. Joseph's risk paid off, just as mine did. Jesus was not an ordinary man but one that would resurrect. Joseph discovered the Resurrection power of Jesus Christ: it is the power to change a Pharisee into a follower. And it is the power to help even an enemy become a friend and follower.

QUESTIONS TO THINK ABOUT

1. What is the risk for you to become a follower and join the adventure?

2. What groups are you most afraid to share your faith with?

3. Are you a secret follower? What would it take for you to come out of the closet?

4. Have you ever really given God your all?

5. Have you ever let the Resurrection power of Jesus fill you?

6. What will God do with you if you risk it all and join the adventure?

7. Take a minute and draw a mental picture of where you think God will have taken you ten years from now.

Four

The Pharisees in My Church

While crawling through a field on our hands and knees, my wife and I suddenly realize that bears are surrounding us. I watch Audrey shake with adrenaline. Her hands clutch her rifle, ready for action. Her face is flush, and her eyes continually shift as she watches the bears. I feel the adrenaline rush, too: feeding fifty yards on our left is a 300-pound bear, on our right is a 250-pound one, in front is another 250-pound bear with a white spot on its chest, and behind—moving our way—is another 300-pound black bear. We are surrounded! Any sudden move might reveal our presence. It would take a bear less than three seconds to charge in if he wanted to. One swipe of the paw could disembowel us. One bite on the back of the neck could be paralyzing. This is life is at its best!

AUDREY'S FIRST BEAR

Every year, my wife and I plan a new adventure together. Although some are more dangerous than others, I try to choose one in hopes that she will come along. With her consent, I picked moose and bear hunting in British Columbia.

We sought out a guide at the local sportsman show. After interviewing each one, we found one we thought would be perfect. We anticipated this adventure all year.

We love eating wild game. We find it to be healthier meat, and it is exciting and challenging to harvest an animal and bring it to the table. Almost every day, we eat some type of wild game. This trip would give us adventure and wild game; bear meat is outstanding if cooked correctly, and moose meat is the best of all the deer family. Audrey makes a bear chili that is to die for—I just don't want to die to get it.

We arrived early in the day and met our guide at the lodge. He had been scouting a nearby field and suggested we start hunting immediately. We drove to the field and then climbed into the back of the pickup to spot for bears. We saw what we were looking for while standing and glassing the field; there was a black bear about three hundred yards away from us. He was feeding in the waist-tall, ready-to-harvest oat field. We watched the bear as he used his fingers to strip the oats right into his mouth. This would be the perfect time for Audrey to harvest her first bear.

Audrey began to shake in anticipation. My wife has always surprised me with how much she likes big-game hunting. She loves spotting game and evaluating it. She loves being in the woods and enjoying God's creation. And she loves her daily hot shower, so this outfitter provided it all—it was perfect. We needed to get closer, so we crawled through the oat field on our hands and knees. Our objective was to harvest a mature bear. We would hope for a large boar (male bear). A bear is one of the hardest animals to judge in size, and it is almost impossible to determine sex. We needed to be sure this was a bear without cubs and a mature animal. We moved through the field quietly and slowly. It seemed like forever until we were finally within one hundred yards. Our guide was still not sure if this was the right bear, so we crawled another fifty yards for a closer look. You have to be so careful with movement and sound when you are this close.

Our guide whispered, "Hey, there is another bear." We slowly looked up and fifty yards away, to our left, was a second bear that had entered the field while we were crawling. I looked around and discovered that there was a third bear behind us, following our path into the field. He was one hundred yards away and closing. I looked to the right and discovered a fourth bear at seventy-five yards. We realized we were completely surrounded. I have to say I was more than a little excited. I looked over at Audrey and saw that she was shaking. Adrenaline was coursing through the veins of both of us—we felt so alive! Any sudden move could endanger us. We had to choose quickly— one of these bears would soon stumble onto us.

We knew these black bears could charge us. I have learned that if attacked by a grizzly bear, you should play dead, and eventually he will leave you alone. Many people have chosen this behavior, and it has saved their lives. If a grizzly thinks you're dead, he will bury you and dig you up later when your carcass ripens a bit. A grizzly likes meat aged with a really good bacteria softening up the carcass. However, if a black bear attacks, you have to fight back. He will not leave you alone. Some people have used their fists to fend off an attack. When a black bear kills, he enjoys fresh meat and will eat his fill on the spot. If any of the black bears surrounding us chose to charge, we had to be ready to fight.

We intently watched and waited for each of the bear's next moves. I wondered if Audrey could shoot straight even though she was shaking with excitement. I have missed a number of harvest opportunities because of adrenaline. Just the year before this hunt, I could not stop shaking as I tried to place my cross hairs on a monster mule deer. As adrenaline took over my body, the deer simply walked away.

Finally, we had what we'd come for—the guide pointed, and we noticed a fifth bear. "That's the one," he said. The bear

Audrey after her perfect shot.

An exceptional, follow-up shot to Audrey's perfect shot.

Audrey and me after a long, heart-pounding day in the great outdoors.

was just entering the field. He had a white heart-shaped mark on his chest. Audrey took her time and squeezed the trigger. The other bears—not really knowing what had happened—scrambled in all directions, thankfully not ours. Our freezer would be full of bear meat—it was a perfect shot.

Our soul is made for adventure. You may not like to bear hunt, but God has a leadership adventure for you—He has designed it with you in mind. It will be more than you can handle, but He is your guide. He will be there. If you join Him, you need to know this: sometimes you will be surrounded by modern-day Pharisees, like the ones Jesus faced. Watch how Jesus handled these Pharisees.

SURROUNDED ON THE SABBATH

It was in a grain field that Jesus found himself surrounded.

One Sabbath day as Jesus was walking through some grain fields, His disciples began breaking off heads of grain to eat. But the Pharisees said to Jesus, "Look, why are they breaking the law by harvesting grain on the Sabbath?"(Mark 2:23-24)

Why are the Pharisees following Jesus in a grain field on the Sabbath? Don't they have more to do than that? Aren't they in charge of 480 synagogues? This is game day for them. Shouldn't they be teaching somewhere? It seems obvious to me that Jesus, the new rabbi, was way more popular than they expected. Their job was to protect the laws and the culture they lived in. So, Jesus was their target. He was always surrounded by Pharisees. He was not one of them, so it was just a matter of time before He would break one of their manmade rules. But His disciples broke their law first. The Pharisees expected Jesus to rebuke His disciples and come under their leadership. Instead, this is what happened.

Then Jesus said to them, "The Sabbath was made to meet the needs of people, and not people to meet the requirements of the Sabbath. So the Son of Man is Lord, even over the Sabbath!"(Mark 2:27-28)

This is not what they wanted to hear. The Pharisees were serious about the Sabbath. They worked really hard at making sure everyone else didn't work. They were the Sabbath cops, and their job started Friday night at six o'clock and ended Saturday night at six o'clock. The Sabbath was one of their important doctrines. They believed it was a covenant. Since the name Pharisee means "set apart" and Sabbath means "holy, set apart, reserved for God," the Sabbath was sort of a namesake to them. Over the years, rabbis had tried to answer the question that nobody was asking: what does it mean to rest from work and make this day holy? They had developed thirty-nine different categories of not working for their laws to fall under. Thirty-nine categories turned into hundreds of detailed laws and then into thousands. It was impossible to keep up unless you were a Pharisee. They were obsessed with the Sabbath. If you broke their laws, watch out. The Sabbath had become less of a day of worship and more of a day to dread. Jesus was about to fire a volley in their direction. "The Sabbath was made for man, not man for the Sabbath." Jesus confronted His Pharisees when He claimed to be "Lord of the Sabbath." How in the world did this sincere group of leaders get so far off track? Let's look at the Sabbath and its beginnings. This is one of the oldest known laws.

On the seventh day, God had finished His work of creation, so He rested from all His work. And God blessed the seventh day and declared it holy, because it was the day when He rested from all His work of creation. (Genesis 2:2-3)

What does Genesis teach us about the Sabbath? First, God finished His work and He rested from His creation. The Sabbath is something we step into, not grow into. We step into God's finished work. Second, this day has no morning and no evening. It is a day that has no beginning or ending. The Sabbath is the adventure. Third, the focus is on God resting from creating, not *our* resting. Fourth, it points to the work that would be done on the cross. "It is finished!" Jesus said, and the Sabbath began. The Sabbath points to the cross. They (the Father, Son, and Holy Spirit) finished their work on the cross and created a new life for us.

The next place the Sabbath shows up is in Exodus. The Sabbath was confirmed as one of the Ten Commandments.

You have six days each week for your ordinary work, but the seventh day must be a Sabbath day of complete rest, a holy day dedicated to the LORD. Anyone who works on the Sabbath must be put to death. The people of Israel must keep the Sabbath day by observing it from generation to generation. This is a covenant obligation for all time. (Exodus 31:15-16)

Exodus tells us that this was a life-or-death issue. God was serious about the Sabbath. The Pharisees made it a life-or-death issue, too. The day is about complete rest. I get the sense of the peace that we need to experience by discovering the adventure God has created for us. The day is holy (set apart), reserved for God, not because He needs us, but because we need Him. It is a covenant. It is a promise that points to the cross. That is why Jesus said, "The Son of Man is Lord of the Sabbath." There is much more about the Sabbath in the Old Testament, and you can see why the Pharisees actually believed they were doing what God wanted. They were zealots for His law. That's why Jesus was always surrounded by Pharisees on the Sabbath. It made adventuring with Him a dangerous situation.

So the Jewish leaders began harassing Jesus for breaking the Sabbath rules. But Jesus replied, "My Father is always working, and so am I." So the Jewish leaders tried all the harder to find a way to kill Him. For He not only broke the Sabbath, He called God His Father, thereby making Himself equal with God. (John 5:16–18)

It is amazing to me that the Sabbath rules are what put Jesus on the cross. The Pharisees had really lost perspective and could not see that the real meaning of the Sabbath was right in front of them. Jesus was the rest. He was the finished work.

So, what was the right perspective, the one the Pharisees were lacking? The apostle Paul, who was a radically converted Pharisee, explains.

So don't let anyone condemn you for what you eat or drink, or for not celebrating certain holy days or new moon ceremonies or Sabbaths. For these rules are only shadows of the reality yet to come. And Christ Himself is that reality. (Colossians 2:16–17)

Jesus is the fulfillment of this law. He is the rest our soul desperately needs. Hebrews explains it clearly.

We know it is ready because of the place in the Scriptures where it mentions the seventh day: "On the seventh day God rested from all His work." But in the other passage God said, "They will never enter My place of rest." (Hebrews 4:4–5)

This rest is God's place, and you cannot find it in a day. You find it in a person named Jesus.

So God's rest is there for people to enter, but those who first heard this good news failed to enter because they disobeyed God. So God set another time for entering His rest, and that time is today. Now if Joshua [he is a type of Christ] had succeeded in giving them this rest, God would not have spoken about another day of rest still to come. So there is a special rest still waiting for the people of God. For all who have entered into God's rest have rested from their labors, just as God did after creating the world. (Hebrews 4:6–10)

God has done work for us through Christ on the cross. He was put on the cross because of the Sabbath. He became the Sabbath for us. It was a life-or-death issue. The work we need in our souls is done on the cross. We find forgiveness of sins not through our work, but through Jesus's work. We step into the rest our souls need. He becomes our Sabbath. It is not a day. Listen to Jesus's message, and you will understand.

Then Jesus said, "Come to Me, all of you who are weary and carry heavy burdens, and I will give you rest. Take My yoke upon you. Let Me teach you, because I am humble and gentle at heart, and you will find rest for your souls. For My yoke is easy to bear, and the burden I give you is light." (Matthew 11:28–30)

The rest we need from the Sabbath is not a day, but a yoke. The yoke Jesus is speaking of is a wooden yoke that connects two oxen together as they pull a cart. The picture is clear. When you pull the cart alone, you will never find rest. When you join in His yoke, you will find the rest your soul longs for. This rest is the moment in your life that you give Jesus complete control.

SUMMERTIME SABBATH

The news about our Mill Creek church plant had spread. There was a genuine interest in our story. We had grown from our core group of ten to over five hundred people in just five years. We had a creative group that pushed the edge to discover new ways of reaching people. Because of the rapid growth, I was invited to speak at a gathering of pastors in Missouri. I knew my story of God's grace and the miracle of how God helped us start the church would be inspiring. I hoped that my "Only God" story would inspire an "Only God" story in them. Because 80 percent of pastors in attendance were leading declining churches, they really wanted to learn how to turn things around. At least that's what I hoped.

I shared the miracle story of how our church got started. I could not help but cry and give God the glory for what He had done and what He was doing. I chose to share a story of my struggle in the first year.

I told about the five families, my core group, that agreed to help me start the church, who were not all Christians. Summer was approaching, and in meeting with the planning committee of our church, I was trying to figure out how to survive the first summer. When talking with them, I realized they had no plans to attend church in the summer. For them, summer weekends were for camping and fun in the sun. They had no solution for the problem. My core group was going away. I didn't know what to do. We had just started, and now it appeared that we would fail in the first summer.

Then, I had an idea. I suggested we move Sunday morning worship to Wednesday night. I would set up camping trips for the church, and we would cancel our Sunday morning services all summer. We started a summer adventure for us that included taking Sundays off every summer.

I told the group of pastors that for three years, I did not attend church on Sundays during the summertime. This innovative idea actually saved our church.

Not realizing it, the pastors had become Pharisees—when I looked up, they were ready to attack. I could feel the temperature in the room escalate. They did not listen to any more of my ideas. All they heard was that I didn't go to church on Sundays for three summers.

Suddenly, one of the pastors-turned-Pharisees stood and interrupted me. He pointed his finger at me and condemned me for taking Sundays off. He cited the Fourth Commandment: the Sabbath was holy, and I was not. He was sure I was sinning. He lectured me. Another stood and added to it, and then another. I was surrounded. Before the meeting was over, they had discounted everything I had shared. Ideas that could have helped them out of their decline were dismissed because of their Sabbath beliefs. Somehow, they had lost their perspective and didn't understand what the Sabbath really was.

That day did not end well. The leader who had invited me was in trouble with these pastors-turned-Pharisees. I was quickly ushered back to the airport. Someone needed to confront these Pharisees. I was hoping that Jesus would show up.

God is not interested in our worship for one day. He wants to lead us on an adventure. The Sabbath we need is found in surrender to His yoke. I believe that as you surrender, He will fill you with His power through the Holy Spirit. Many people have discovered the rest that comes from the cross. We step into His finished work called salvation. But there is more: don't stop discovering the rest that comes when you surrender. Jesus is the Sabbath we need.

QUESTIONS TO THINK ABOUT

1. Have you discovered the rest from the cross?
2. Do you remember that moment of peace?
3. Do you need to step into Jesus's rest and discover forgiveness and grace?
4. Have you surrendered your will?
5. What is the one thing you are holding back?
6. What are you afraid of?
7. What do you now believe the Sabbath is?
8. What needs rest in your life?

Five

The Pharisees in My Camp

I'm nearly asleep. It's been a long week hiking up and down the mountains searching for elk. I lean back, propped up against a log, facing the hillside with the wind in my face. I cannot be more relaxed. From the corner of my eye, I sense something. There's movement. Six yards from me is a huge black bear that's snuck up from behind. I'm shocked that it has come so close to me, and without my knowing it. If I panic, it could elicit an attack. My rifle is six feet away from me, lying in the grass. My heart is beating out of my chest; I am frozen in fear. This is a life-and-death situation.

WHEN A BEAR SNEAKS UP ON YOU

On this hunting trip, my friend Steve graciously allowed a group of us from church to use his cabins in Camas Creek, Idaho. The log cabins sit on the edge of the Frank Church-River of No Return Wilderness Area near Camas, Idaho. This was an ideal spot to hunt—a perfect habitat for elk and deer.

After forty-five miles on an increasingly narrow gravel road, we arrived at the even narrower dirt road that would take us to the cabins. A full-size truck is too wide for this road; it is made for a Jeep or small four-wheel-drive pickup. Those who choose to take a full-size truck up the road end up with body damage from the brush and have to stop occasionally to build up the road on the steep sides of the hills or they will slide fifty to one hundred feet into the creek.

We unlocked a gate and started the eight-mile drive through rivers and up and down steep roads. The road led to cabins, which were an old hunting camp. Because of wilderness restrictions, the public has to hike or travel by horseback to get to the starting point, where Steve's cabins are located. The local hunters were envious because this privilege was not available to them.

The trip into camp was an adventure in itself. Sometimes at the Camas Creek crossing, the water gets so high that it seeps into the floorboards of the vehicle. The blind corners of the steep roads also keep you guessing. If you guess wrong, you'll drive right off the edge and fall forty feet to the creek bottom. There is a sign at each corner commemorating someone who made the wrong turn. While they did not lose their lives, they often lost their vehicles. The creek level was medium high, and we drove off the road only once as we made our way in.

We set up camp in the cabins and prepared for the weeklong hunt. Our permits allowed us to harvest either a bull elk or a cow elk. The altitude of our cabins was 5,000 feet; each day we hiked up to the 9,500-foot peaks. However, there were no elk or deer in sight.

The reintroduction of wolves into this area of Idaho had had a big impact. Studies in Yellowstone showed that one wolf kills an average of seventeen elk per year if they're available or about forty-four deer per year if they're available. Wolves are known to be opportunistic killers—if they find a herd wallowing in high snow, they will kill the entire herd.

Their nature makes them kill for food and for fun. Wolves have reduced the big-game population, especially elk, because that's their favorite food. The Camas Creek area normally has large herds of deer and elk, but the wolves made it very different that year. In previous years, we could always count on finding deer in the ravines and draws, but they were gone. This was discouraging to all of us. It seemed that I would have to go home and explain to my wife and family why I spent over one thousand dollars in tags and travel and had nothing to show for it. Hunters call this "eating your tag"—it leaves a bad taste in your mouth.

Even though we didn't have much luck finding game, I enjoyed—as I always do—being out in the woods. Hunting restores my soul. I am reminded that life on earth is only temporary. There's something special about being in the mountains and waking up with five inches of snow on your tent. Something about sleeping in a tent with temperatures close to zero, waking up when it's still dark to get to a look out at first light. Something about stumbling into camp after dark—exhausted after a long day—and starting a fire to take the chill off. You cannot imagine the skies at night, high in the mountains. You feel as if you can just touch the sky. However, something new happened on this trip.

We planned to get up early for a daybreak hunt, so we spiked out our tent in an eight-thousand-foot saddle. The zero-degree night had frozen our water solid. We thawed our pans of water on the hiking stove to cook oatmeal and make coffee. In the early hours, deer and elk move about more, so it's best to be in an area with a good view and stay there until the cold forces you to walk to get warm.

I was too cold to stay in one place, so I was hiking around the hills when I heard wolves. They were miles away, but were in our same drainage. They were also looking for elk and deer. They howled, talking back and forth to each other as they traveled. I made my way through the thick timber and skirted the side of the mountain. My friend Jim was hunting with me that day. We were one thousand yards apart when the howling got louder. The sound of wolves in the wilderness actually raises the hair on the back of your neck. These animals are truly amazing. They add a new element to the wilderness that brings a thrill to my soul. As I listened to them howl, I realized the pack was heading toward me. The wolves were no longer just in our drainage; they were in my draw, less than five hundred yards away. I started to rethink my position. Within ten minutes, they surrounded me and were howling back and forth to each other. I could tell they were within fifty yards. They were so close, yet I could not see them. "Eerie" is the only word I can think of to describe the moment.

It was as if the wolves were looking at me, deciding if they should eat me. As a precaution, I put a shell in the chamber of my rifle and moved backward toward a tree. I cannot say I was afraid. It was exhilarating—well worth the one thousand dollars I paid for the tags on this trip. I was ready to protect myself if they did attack but would have to deal with questions and paperwork if I shot one. Thankfully, the wolves moved on, determining that I was not worth the effort.

I called Jim on our radios and asked him to come over. He had heard the howling too, so we decided to stick together. As we hiked along once again, the pack surrounded us; the wolves were checking us out. There was no question—this pack was deciding what it was going to do with us. I have heard only a few cases where wolves have attacked and killed people. However, if hungry enough, they could become aggressive and try to make a meal out of us. Again, the wolves decided to move on to try to find the elk herd. We were not on their menu that day. We spent the rest of the day in the woods, walking with a little more caution than usual.

The end of the week came quickly, and we never saw any elk or deer. On our last evening to hunt, I packed up the high camp and hiked 4,500 feet down toward the cabin. Since we had not seen any big game, my expectations were diminishing. That evening, I set up for the last hunt at the base of a hillside. I sat there waiting for the sun to go down on my hunt. I laid my rifle on the ground, leaned against a log, and started to doze, exhausted from a long day of hiking.

Then, I felt its presence. I turned my head around slowly; there was something behind me. It was a large black bear, and he was

Camp at seven thousand feet where we spent a week.

almost on top of me! There was no time to think, my instincts took over. I dove for my rifle, yelling at the bear. The sudden movement could have provoked an attack, but instead, I startled the bear. I picked up the rifle, ready to shoot, but the bear took off running. Remember, a bear can run thirty miles an hour for short distances, and I was thankful that the direction was away from—and not toward—me. I had a bear tag, but I couldn't find him in the scope fast enough. When I realized what had happened, I started shaking with adrenaline. The reality was I almost killed him and he almost killed me.

On all my adventures, I have found that the most dangerous bear is the one you don't know is there. When following Jesus on the adventure He has for you, you have to watch out for bears—especially the bear that is right next to you.

BETRAYED BY A CLOSE FRIEND

Then Jesus said, "I chose the twelve of you, but one is a devil." He was speaking of Judas, son of Simon Iscariot, one of the Twelve, who would later betray Him. (John 6:70–71)

This was a teaching moment for Jesus. He was teaching His disciples how to confront the Pharisee right next to them—the one they didn't know about. Jesus had been noticing a change in Judas for a while. We know that Judas had begun to steal from the treasury. It is always these disciples-turned-Pharisees close to us that trip us up the most. We don't expect them. It hurts more than we ever imagined. It seems impossible to have someone so close to you hurt you or betray you. When confronting this Pharisee, most people will lose their way. The "why" questions especially get us. *Why didn't we notice? Why did God allow them in my life? Why would they do this?* And then others follow. *Can I trust my judgment to pick my close friends?*

Let me set the scene for this confrontation. First, let's back up a few verses and look at what had just happened.

So Jesus said again, "I tell you the truth, unless you eat the flesh of the Son of Man and drink His blood, you cannot have eternal life within you. But anyone who eats My flesh and drinks My blood has eternal life, and I will raise that person at the last day. For My flesh is true food, and My blood is true drink. Anyone who eats My flesh and drinks My blood remains in Me, and I in him. (John 6:53–56)

These were hard words for the disciples to understand. We now know Jesus was talking about communion and the cross. They heard only the impossible-to-understand thought of cannibalism. Even as I read, it is hard to comprehend what Jesus meant at the time. His leadership in our lives will lead us to places and experiences we don't understand. The disciples were shocked.

Many of His disciples said, "This is very hard to understand. How can anyone accept it?" Jesus was aware that His disciples were complaining, so He said to them, "Does this offend you?" (John 6:60-61)

When you are complaining or are offended, the question is: what will you do? When God leads you somewhere you don't want to go, what will you do? Jesus was leading them to the cross. No one wants to go there. But that is where He will lead every one of us on our adventure. On the way to the cross, you discover the Pharisee who is unwilling to go.

Jesus explained His words.

"The Spirit alone gives eternal life. Human effort accomplishes nothing. And the very words I have spoken to you are spirit and life. But some of you do not believe Me." (For Jesus knew from the beginning which ones didn't believe, and He knew who would betray Him.) (John 6:63-64)

Jesus was talking about Judas, who was standing right behind him, holding the money for the band of disciples. Judas was sneaking up on Him. You will have a moment like that too. One day it will shake you to the core. A good, trusted disciple will become a Pharisee that is ready to destroy you. What will you do?

At this point many of His disciples turned away and deserted Him. Then Jesus turned to the Twelve and asked, "Are you also going to leave?" (John 6:66-67)

Some are surprised that Jesus did not go after the deserters and explain His words more clearly or give them a second chance. Instead, He did nothing. Jesus was a leader. He was on the way to the cross—and it takes complete trust to get there. I often do not understand where His adventure for me is headed. I can imagine Him asking me the same question when I complain, "Are you also going to leave?" It is easy to be like those who abandoned Him.

Simon Peter replied, "Lord, to whom would we go? You have the words that give eternal life. We believe, and we know You are the Holy One of God." (John 6:68-69)

I love Peter's answer. "I know You, but I don't understand this." The truth is every disciple deserted Jesus in the end. We all have to own our tendency to desert. Leaders understand that God will never take free will from us. I have seen people walk away from Jesus when it got rough and return to the life they had before. It is sad because they did not see what God had in store for them.

As soon as they arrived, Judas walked up to Jesus. "Rabbi!" he exclaimed, and gave Him the kiss. (Mark 14:45)

Then all His disciples deserted Him and ran away. (Mark 14:50)

It is sad to think that one of Jesus's closest, most trusted disciples betrayed Him. It is even more profound to think that every disciple has deserted Him. Including us.

WHEN CLOSE FRIENDS SNEAK UP

Last night, I heard about a couple that left our church; they had been good members. I knew them by name and knew their kids. When they had a crisis, I responded and counseled their daughter. I invested numerous hours into this family. I made sure their children had a great Christian education and helped them connect with a small group. They would often tell me how much they loved the sermons and the church. But sometimes those who sneak up behind us are the ones we least expect. Sometimes they don't have our best interests in mind.

When they left, they told their friends it was because they did not understand where the money went that they tithed. They implied that we were not spending God's money correctly. This saddened me. They had never asked anyone questions about this or mentioned any doubts they had. They had my number; I had responded to them every time they called. I do not believe this was the real issue at all. It is almost never what is first said. They also said I told too many stories in my messages and the church was getting too big. Unfortunately, I will never know the real reason why they left. I am not sure even they know. Pharisees in your camp will often point at you, rather than examine themselves. It is really hard to look honestly at yourself in the mirror.

Through my thirty years of leadership as a pastor, I have learned that people come and go. I have also learned to hold onto people I love with open hands. When someone walks away, it reminds me of the One I work for. It reminds me to have confidence in the One who calls the shots. God has called me to a mission: I am to take as many people with me to Heaven as I can. If someone walks away from the church, it is sad to me; but if the person also walks away from God, it is devastating. This mission sometimes takes me to the cross.

Many see me as a self-assured leader with no fear. What they do not know is that there are times when self-doubt sneaks up on me and tries to kill my confidence. If successful, then it has become about me. I become scared into believing that the direction God has given me is wrong. If I allow this to happen, then I am dead.

Too many pastors leave ministry because of the Pharisees that sneak up on them. One thousand seven hundred pastors a month leave the ministry. Statistics from Pastoral Care, Inc.

state that 50 percent of pastors polled say they would leave the ministry if they could. The devastating toll on these religious leaders leaves them feeling less valuable than when they started. It is easy to let yourself slip into desertion.

When people make the choice to leave our church, I find that if I spend too much time asking "why" it will kill me and kill the church that God has asked me to build. It's impossible for someone to understand completely what it feels like when people leave because of what you say or how you lead. I am tempted to turn to everyone else, and like Jesus, ask, "Are you also going to leave?" But I have learned that the real question I have to ask is "what?" What am I to do with all of this? What is it you want, Lord? It is not about me. If people leave, should I panic, run, quit, become paralyzed? What happens next? Whose words will I listen to? Mine filled with doubts, those of my Pharisees, or the words of my Lord?

As for the couple, it's unfortunate that the relationship we'd built with their family wasn't enough to get them to stay. There were things I wanted to say to them, things like: "The church's financial books are open. You can see where all the money goes." Or, "Pentecost had three thousand come to church on the first day. Is that too big?" Or, "Jesus was a storyteller—that is how people learn." I did not have the opportunity to say those things to them. They were long gone and had no intention of talking with me. So I just said them in my mind. Maybe that helped me.

If I am going to follow Jesus into this leadership adventure, there will be times some will not understand what we are doing. There will be times I will not always understand, but I will not be afraid of the Pharisee who sneaks up behind or beside me. Jesus was 100 percent human and 100 percent God. I know in His humanness He asked to avoid the cross as He knelt in the garden. I wonder about those painful hours He had all alone. I wonder if He felt the pain of failure and the pain of people leaving Him. I wonder if that is where those drops of blood came from as He prayed. I think He understands everyone who is blindsided by a Pharisee. Today, though, I want to be able to say with Simon Peter, "Lord, to whom would we go? You have the words that give eternal life." I would rather follow Jesus to a cross I don't understand than to choose my own way.

We ask the question "why" more often than we ask "what." The "whys" of life pile up, and if we do not understand, we blame God and quit following. Judas quit following completely. He never was able to forgive himself or accept God's forgiveness. Every other disciple had to deal with his own desertion. Each one had to accept the grace of God and discover the power of the cross that changes. Who will you be?

QUESTIONS TO THINK ABOUT

1. Have you been hurt deeply by someone close?

2. Have you let it affect you and keep you from following?

3. Have your "whys" piled up?

4. Have you asked "what?"

5. Have you asked, "What do You want me to do now?"

6. Have you asked, "What can You do with my brokenness?"

7. How have you deserted someone?

8. How have you hurt someone?

9. Can you trust God to lead you, even when you don't understand?

Six

The Pharisees
in My Community

Our Canadian guide Dan, Dominic, and I drive up a trail in the Alberta wilderness. We're driving in an Argo, an eight-wheel-drive, land/water, all-terrain vehicle because it's the only way to get around in that wilderness. We've tagged out on moose and are ready to help Dominic find a good bear. As we travel along, I look up and see him—a cinnamon-phase black bear. He's small, about four feet long, two hundred pounds. He sits in the middle of the road on a pile of leaves—his food cache. He looks determined to protect it. With his head down, he swings it back and forth, huffing as we near. We stop the Argo, get out, and approach him. Abandoning our good judgment, we walk over to him. As we get closer, I realize that none of us has brought a gun! What are we thinking? We're less than twenty-five yards away from this bear!

MEET BOZO

In October 2013, I went on a moose-hunting trip with my friend Dominic. We chose an outfitter in Northern Alberta, Canada. Dominic was excited about this trip! I wasn't. I've gone moose hunting four times and left empty-handed four times. It cost me a bunch. I planned to enjoy an adventure with my friend but had no expectations of success. Dominic was convinced that this time we would be successful. I needed his confidence because I had none.

The area where we would hunt in Northern Alberta has moose, black bears, and grizzly bears. We traveled twenty hours north of Seattle and left our trucks at a drop-off point. We then drove by Argo for four hours on a trail through tundra and beaver swamps to reach camp.

During the first few days, we had great success with our moose hunt. Dominic scored first, shooting a moose that was called to within fifteen yards. We celebrated! I was happy that someone on one of my moose hunts finally scored. I was even more surprised when our guide, Dan, called in a fifty-four-inch moose right next to me. The moose towered over me with a thick band of brush in-between us. The only things I could see were his antlers. He stepped to the side, and at fifteen yards, I shot him through the heart. I had finally harvested the very thing that had always eluded me.

Finally, a moose!

Dominic and me on the way into our camp.

It took us until midnight to clean and quarter him for transport to camp. While quartering him, I laid my knife down and stepped back, lifting a quarter of the moose in my hands. The knife blade had tipped up, and I drove the knife into my ankle, right through the boot. This made the rest of the night a little more interesting.

After dressing the wound the next morning, we made plans for the rest of the week. We would shoot grouse and find a first bear for Dominic. We were enjoying this wilderness experience, taking in God's creation.

The next day, we removed all the scraps of meat left over from the moose hanging in our camp. We placed the scraps in a small aluminum trailer that hauls gear behind the Argo. When the Argo floats a beaver pond, the trailer is watertight and floats behind it. As we came around the corner, we saw him—the cinnamon-phase black bear. He sat on his food cache, blocking the road. We'd heard stories about this particular bear from our camp mates.

While Dominic and I were out hunting with our guide the day before, the camp cook and a guide with another

The Argo and trailer ready to be loaded.

hunter had run into this bear and named him Bozo. They'd videotaped him crawling into their trailer while they were trying to get rid of scraps. Bozo showed no fear. He was a young bear and had not been hunted or had any experiences with humans. He spent almost an hour eating scraps a few feet from the staff. He was too small to harvest. When we came

Encountering Bozo on his food cache.

upon the bear, I smiled when I looked at him—he did look like a Bozo.

We drove up close to his cache and got out. We saw that Bozo had buried the uneaten scraps he'd gotten from the camp staff the day before. We wanted to see how close we could get. The friendly Bozo of the trailer incident was not so friendly anymore. He clearly had an attitude.

Even at his relatively small size for a bear—four feet, two hundred pounds—Bozo had ten times the strength of a man and could sprint at thirty miles an hour. Since no one had bothered to bring a rifle, our guide picked up a couple of sticks to make noise in case Bozo didn't think we were funny and decided to charge. We stopped fifteen feet from him. There we stood, facing this bear, armed with only sticks. I'm not sure what we were thinking. Bozo was agitated, snapping his jaw and moving his head from side to side.

Back to the Argo we headed. To my surprise, Dan drove the vehicle right on top of Bozo's food cache and stopped. I guess he thought it would be entertaining to watch Bozo's reaction—and ours. He was not disappointed. Bozo had moved twenty feet off the trail but then returned to his food cache. He was angry that we had parked right on top of his food. We were nervous and a little fearful that our guide had stopped on top of it, too. As Bozo got closer, Dan just laughed. Bozo was now six feet away and noticed the scraps in our trailer. He crawled in and started to eat.

There he was, three feet away! I did my best to keep Dominic—who was in the back of the Argo—between Bozo and me. Dominic tried to crawl into the front with us. I videotaped Bozo eating the scraps. He looked our way two or three times, and we thought he might just continue snacking on us. Dan told us not to make any sudden movements; if we did, we could make Bozo mad. Mad? I thought he already was mad—we were parked on his food cache! Dominic and I were terrified that he might continue the final three feet and

Bozo coming after our scraps less than four feet from us. We are parked on his food cache.

take a bite out of us. Eventually, Dan got tired of the game, and we left to find a bigger bear. But Bozo had certainly made an impression.

Our soul has a guide, too. It is Jesus. And He has a great sense of humor. Jesus often toyed with the Pharisees, much as we toyed with Bozo the bear. I think Jesus wants to see what we will do with the Bozos we run into. In the next story, we see His sense of humor in action.

PLAYING WITH PHARISEES

One day while Jesus was teaching, some Pharisees and teachers of religious law were sitting nearby. (It seemed that these men showed up from every village in all Galilee and Judea, as well as from Jerusalem.) And the Lord's healing power was strongly with Jesus. (Luke 5:17)

The Pharisees were just like Bozo. They always showed up at meal times. They seemed harmless, but they were dangerous. They took up the front-row seats. They were there to judge and watch. They didn't seem to be there to learn. The Lord's healing power was at work, but the Bozos were in the way.

Some men came carrying a paralyzed man on a sleeping mat. They tried to take him inside to Jesus. (Luke 5:18)

There was no room for him. How does this happen? It happens when the Bozos are taking up space. We should never have a situation where there is not room for another lost or hurting person. As our church has gotten larger, it has been harder for some to make room for another broken person. "When is it ever big enough?" someone will say. I think, *How can you even ask that?* I wonder if we should close the door before or after your friend gets in. Or how about your kids or grandkids—should we let them in?

The answer is obvious to me: we need to make room for everyone. Our state has the smallest percentage of Christians in any state; only 10 percent identify themselves as Christians. Most foreign countries have a higher percentage of Christians than the state of Washington. How did it get that way? I see some amazing churches in our area. So what happened? Here is what I think happened. The Bozos are allowed to call the shots, and there is not room for the broken. Over the years, the churches that were full didn't continue to make room. They became content with their crowd and left the hurting, needy person outside.

Now we are such a small percentage that at times we seem irrelevant. But the Bozos are still at it. They say, "I like it small and intimate." I went to a new church plant recently. The pastor told me that his philosophy was to take care of those he had coming to church; someone else would have to make room for the broken. He had no plans for growth. I don't understand that, and I don't think Jesus does either.

But they couldn't reach Him because of the crowd. So they went up to the roof and took off some tiles. Then they lowered the sick man on his mat down into the crowd, right in front of Jesus. (Luke 5:19)

Who were these guys? Why don't we get their names? They had to be friends. They're the kind of friends who carried their paralyzed friend to Jesus. I want that kind of friend! I want to be that kind of friend! They're the ones who stay with me when I am paralyzed with fear or defeated in life. I need that kind of friend. I need to be that kind of friend.

They had to have faith. These men believed if they just got their friend in front of Jesus something would happen. They were the kind of guys who didn't take no for an answer. These were the guys who got things done when no one else did. These guys are the heroes of this story, and we don't even know their names.

Seeing their faith, Jesus said to the man, "Young man, your sins are forgiven." (Luke 5:20)

This is where it happened; Jesus showed His sense of humor. First, I wonder if He was messing with the guys who carried their friend. I think these guys were disappointed. They'd heard about Jesus's healing power, and He said He forgave this man's sins? Did Jesus not see that the man was paralyzed? I honestly think that some people come to Jesus demanding some outside work. When Jesus knows it is much more difficult to heal the inside, He starts there. I can imagine the smile that spread across Jesus's face because He knew what was going to happen next.

But the Pharisees and teachers of religious law said to themselves, "Who does He think He is? That's blasphemy! Only God can forgive sins!" (Luke 5:21)

Jesus was messing with the Bozos. I bet that smile grew as they got wound up. This was fun. Let's see how far He took it.

Jesus knew what they were thinking, so he asked them, "Why do you question this in your hearts?" (Luke 5:22)

Jesus knows what we are thinking. He knows when we are mad. Sometimes I think He even enjoys those moments and wants to teach us something. In this story, He had them all right where He wanted them.

"Is it easier to say 'Your sins are forgiven,' or 'Stand up and walk'? So I will prove to you that the Son of Man has the authority on earth to forgive sins." Then Jesus turned to the paralyzed man and said, "Stand up, pick up your mat, and go home!" And immediately, as everyone watched, the man jumped up, picked up his mat, and went home praising God. (Luke 5: 23-25)

I can imagine the smile on Jesus's face—but there also must have been smiles on the faces of the heroes of this story. I don't think they hung around. I think they walked arm in arm with the friend they'd carried. I wish I could hear their conversation. I wonder if their broken friend thanked them?

Everyone was gripped with great wonder and awe, and they praised God, exclaiming, "We have seen amazing things today!" (Luke 5:26)

Notice what happened here. Everyone was amazed. I am guessing that included the Bozos. Jesus must have laughed out loud at the transformation of even the Bozos. The Bozos who had held so much power became powerless.

MY BOZOS

I met some Bozos when we did a sermon series called Permanent Ink. Our creative team started to think about the large number of people under the age of thirty who sport tattoos. So in this series, we invited people with

From left: The tattoo artist, our church member, and me during the Permanent Ink service.

tattoos to tell their stories each week. We also decided to give someone the opportunity to remove a tattoo if he or she had become ashamed of it. We took a video crew into the doctor's office and recorded the beginning of the long tattoo removal process. We showed it at our Sunday service. It reminded all that they should be sure of what they do in and out of the tattoo chair.

Up until that point, the entire crowd had responded positively to the series. On the final Sunday, we chose to have a visual while the sermon took place. We asked a tattoo artist to join us onstage along with someone from our church who was already planning to get a tattoo. The artist tattooed that person during the message.

The press got wind of it, and we had television coverage from several stations. My message that day was all about how to get your name permanently put into the Book of Life (see Revelation 20:15 and 21:27). We had prepared Bibles to give away and had a guest book for people to sign to symbolically place their names in the Book of Life. I was absolutely moved as fifty-five adults walked down to write their names in ink in the book. This service became the vehicle for them to change their lives. It was powerful and moving.

The Bozos started showing up the next day. The ones who complained were the religious—people who didn't like tattoos and didn't like those who have them. They certainly didn't like a pastor who encouraged someone to get a tattoo. Over the course of several days, these modern-day Pharisees forgot about—or never asked about—the fifty-five people who found Christ. They could not see past their prejudices and instead focused on the tattoos. Here are some of the cleaner comments from our Christian friends who commented on our story in the news. "Some things in the Old Testament still apply to us today as far as obedience goes. Tattoos are rooted in a 'spirit of rebellion' which God condemns under grace just as He did under law." "What a demonic way to appear utterly disconnected from the gospel." "Taking a tattoo is like taking the mark and it is also unbiblical." And finally, this is my favorite: "B.S. Report—Pastor Kellogg sounds like a real cornflake to me." The comments went on and on until friends actually called me, worried about how I was taking all of it. I assured them I was okay—I reminded them that those comments came from Bozos.

Christian radio hosts, who promised to let me share what happened, also contacted me. When the program started, I was talked over and derided for what we did. One couple in our church wrote me a note to tell me how unbiblical I was and how terrible the tattooing was. I was disappointed that they would not sit down with me to hear what really happened. They had not even been there to witness the service—they never even knew about the fifty-five. Some members of our church left to find a church that didn't push out to the edge to reach people with tattoos. Maybe they settled into one of those churches that are full. I am okay that they left; they made room for more broken people.

The Bozos we met through that series just made me smile. They were mad at me. They were self-righteous keepers of the law who missed what was really happening in the hearts of those who found Christ. It makes me wonder: since tattoos are a little more accepted these days, how many of those same people now sport tattoos? My wife plans to get one on her foot to remind her of our recent accomplishment of summiting Mount Kilimanjaro. I wonder if she will be the next target of the Bozos?

We saw fifty-five people come forward to write their names that day. Who can honestly argue with the power of God to transform a person? The greatest evidence that there is a God is that He continues to transform broken people—even the Bozos.

QUESTIONS TO THINK ABOUT

Who are you in the story?

1. Are you the friend who has tenacity and faith to bring someone to Jesus and see what happens?

2. Are you the disappointed?

3. Are you the one who can't see what God is doing on the inside and who is asking Him to do something on the outside?

4. Are you the Bozo hanging onto your power, more interested in judging than following?

5. Are you the paralytic on the way home, praising God because of all He has done?

I don't know about you, but I find myself in all those characters from time to time. I just don't want to stay as any of them for long—unless it is the friend.

Seven

The Blind Pharisees

Two young bears cling to two trees near me. They're crying to their mother. It is eerie! The sound is like the cry of a distressed baby. I am shaking with the effects of adrenaline. I hear the huff of the mother bear nearby. You can hear the mother bear pawing at the ground, getting ready to charge. I smell the strong, musky scent of the angry mother bear. My plan was to help my friend—now I am the one in need of help. I place a shell in the chamber and await the charge.

A HORSEBACK RIDE AND BEING CALLED INTO HARM'S WAY

My brother Ron invited me along on a horseback trip into the wilderness of the Cascade Mountains. It was September, and the ten-day early buck season was in full swing. I brought my friend Jim for a weeklong trip in the high country of the Cascades. We were looking for a mature mule deer or a bear—both seasons were open. We traveled by horse along Icicle Creek. We stopped at the bridge where a man had lost his life earlier that year. The man's horse was frightened and stumbled on the bridge, plunging them into the water below, to his death. The horse stood by his deceased owner until a hiker passed by. Riding horses on a hunt saves your legs, but it can also create new challenges. We were traveling

French Ridge and its narrow trails.

along the creek bottom to a trail that led up to French Ridge. We made our way to the high country, above the tree line, and near the peaks of unnamed mountains in the Cascade Range.

These hunting trips add fuel to my soul. I love to push the limits of my ability. I had never really traveled much by horseback, and here I was, going eighteen miles into the high-country wilderness. The trail up the ridge is steep and very narrow at times.

When packing into a camp, it takes about one horse per hunter to carry general camp gear and personal gear. We had three packhorses and two riding horses. Jim was hiking along without a pack. Our first adventure mishap happened just outside the valley when our packhorse didn't watch where she was going; she simply walked off the edge of the steep trail and rolled part way down the mountain with two very full packs on her packsaddles. I knew that if the horse was injured it would be the end of the trip. Horses can lose their lives this way; when they're injured and unable to move, you have no choice but to put them out of their misery. We unpacked her while she lay precariously on the side of a very steep mountain. One wrong move and she would roll two thousand feet to the bottom and die.

Ron, Jim, and I pulled her to her feet and then pushed and pulled with all we had to get her back up the hill to the trail. At one point, the horse actually blacked out. We had to keep her from rolling all the way down the hill until she was able to get back on her feet. After fighting our way back onto the trail and reloading her, we pushed onto the high mountain camp. This experience added a little excitement to the trip. I began to wonder if my horse would just walk off the hill and then we'd both have to be put out of our misery at the bottom.

We planned to hunt deer above the tree line where bucks whose antlers are in velvet hang out until their antlers harden. Washington has an early high hunt that allows you to hunt both bear and deer above the tree line in the wilderness. The deer are spread out, and it's very difficult to find them. But my brother and I love the experience of the high-country hunt, even though we are not successful most of the time.

Our group decided to split up for the morning hunt. Jim and I took off up the valley, hunting our way to the top of a ridge one thousand feet above us. The morning was cold but sunny and made for great hiking. We enjoyed the beauty of the hunt but didn't see anything. It was midday when we finally arrived at the top of the ridgeline. We were planning to spend the rest of the day in the same valley.

Before we started to hunt back toward camp, we stepped across the ridge to look down the other side at a beautiful bright-blue, crystal-clear lake and the spectacular views from the ridgeline to a series of ridgelines and peaks. As we admired the breathtaking surroundings, we spotted them—three bears about two miles away on the other side of the valley. We were excited to see game. The bears were in the opposite direction of our camp, but we enthusiastically made the decision to go after them. This was my first chance to harvest a bear.

Jim and I were young and ambitious. We decided to run down a very steep mountainside right toward the bears. It was crazy and a little dangerous. I ran toward the area full-blast on a two-mile descent into a valley. I lost my footing twice and cartwheeled down the hill. Unhurt, each time, I got up and kept running. In less than twenty minutes, we had closed the distance on those bears.

We arrived at the spot about three hundred yards from where we'd seen the bears. We should have been able to see them in the meadow across the valley, but they weren't there. We sat down to think about what to do next. Both of us wanted a shot at those bears. Jim had seen them first, so I suggested he sneak through the patch of woods between the clearing and us. We thought maybe the bears were just out of our line of sight. I also thought that Jim might actually scare them into the open and give me a shot. A while after he left, I heard Jim yell to me, "Dan, get in here!" He wasn't far away, but I couldn't see him. "What do you need?" I asked. "Get in here!" he repeated. "Where are you?" "Get in here now!" he said urgently.

Off I went into the woods, following the sound of his cries. When I found him I said, "What's wrong?" "We are surrounded by bears!" I didn't know it, but he had called me into harm's way. I looked up and saw two cubs in the trees right in front of me. They were less than twenty yards away. The cubs were crying for their mom. My system's adrenaline went into overdrive. *What do I do?* I thought. I heard the huffs of the mother bear as she was tearing up a patch of brush, getting ready to make a charge. She was just a few yards away, moving the brush and barking at us. I had no choice: I just backed up to a tree and put a shell in the chamber to wait for the charge. It seemed like forever; we waited, and the bear huffed. Finally, the two cubs dropped to the ground and ran away. A few minutes after that, the mother bear followed. We breathed a collective sigh of relief. Jim was so shaken that his language reverted to some of his pre-Christian days. I looked straight at him and asked, "Why did you call me into harm's way without telling me?" I loved his answer: "You have God on your side. I didn't think He would let anything happen to you!"

On your leadership adventure, your friends will often call you into harm's way. The people you lead cannot see— or understand—what you are doing. They are blind to your leadership. As a leader, you have to know what to do. Jesus was confronted by some very blind, but dangerous, Pharisees.

HEALING THE BLIND

As Jesus was walking along, He saw a man who had been blind from birth. "Rabbi," His disciples asked Him, "Why was this man born blind? Was it because of his own sins or his parents' sins?" (John 9:1-2)

The common teachings of the Pharisees in Jesus's day were that someone was to blame for this man's blindness. They didn't ask, "Can you heal him?" They didn't ask, "What can we do to help him?" They asked "why?" They didn't understand, and sometimes we don't either. I wish there were easy answers, but Jesus gives us a very clear answer.

"It was not because of his sins or his parents' sins," Jesus answered. "This happened so the power of God could be seen in him." (John 9:3)

The impossible makes room for the power of God. I am sad sometimes when I see someone I can't help. What I don't see is what God's power can do to help that person cope with the sickness or use it for His glory.

"We must quickly carry out the tasks assigned us by the One who sent us. The night is coming, and then no one can work. But while I am here in the world, I am the light of the world." Then He spit on the ground, made mud with the saliva, and spread the mud over the blind man's eyes. (John 9:4-6)

This seems to be a cruel joke: spit on the ground, make mud, and spread it on the blind man. Anyone looking on could have been offended. What was Jesus doing?

He told him, "Go wash yourself in the pool of Siloam" (Siloam means "sent"). (John 9:7)

Jesus sent a blind man away with mud on his face. Can you imagine what that looked like? Why would He do that? Why not send one of your disciples to lead him? Why not bring him some water? The "whys" just keep piling up.

So the man went and washed and came back seeing! His neighbors and others who knew him as a blind beggar asked each other, "Isn't this the man who used to sit and beg?" Some said he was, and others said, "No, he just looks like him!" But the beggar kept saying, "Yes, I am the same one!" (John 9:8–9)

The miracle happened, but no one believed. This is funny. It makes me laugh to hear the blind man say, "I am that guy." For years, he had put up with the idea that some sin had caused his blindness. He was looked down upon and snubbed. He then became the miracle that no one could see.

They asked, "Who healed you? What happened?" He told them, "The man they call Jesus made mud and spread it over my eyes and told me, 'Go to the pool of Siloam and wash yourself.' So I went and washed, and now I can see!" "Where is He now?" they asked. "I don't know," he replied. (John 9:10–12)

This seems like a good thing. Where is this miracle worker who heals with mud? But it is a trap.

Then they took the man who had been blind to the Pharisees, because it was on the Sabbath that Jesus had made the mud and healed him. The Pharisees asked the man all about it. So he told them, "He put the mud over my eyes, and when I washed it away, I could see!" Some of the Pharisees said, "This man Jesus is not from God, for He is working on the Sabbath." Others said, "But how

could an ordinary sinner do such miraculous signs?" So there
was a deep division of opinion among them. (John 9:13-16)

Pharisees get stuck looking at the wrong things. They are
blind to the power of God.

Then the Pharisees again questioned the man who had been
blind and demanded, "What's your opinion about this man who
healed you?" The man replied, "I think He must be a prophet."
The Jewish leaders still refused to believe the man had been blind
and could now see, so they called in his parents. They asked
them, "Is this your son? Was he born blind? If so, how can he
now see?" His parents replied, "We know this is our son and that
he was born blind, but we don't know how he can see or who
healed him. Ask him. He is old enough to speak for himself." His
parents said this because they were afraid of the Jewish leaders,
who had announced that anyone saying Jesus was the Messiah
would be expelled from the synagogue. (John 9:17-22)

For the first time, their son was whole. It was not their
sin that had caused his blindness. Their sin would now be
that they were afraid of the wrong people. The Pharisees held
power, but Jesus used His power. Why did they not see His
power? They were officially blind.

That's why they said, "He is old enough. Ask him." So for the
second time they called in the man who had been blind and told
him, "God should get the glory for this, because we know this
man Jesus is a sinner." "I don't know whether He is a sinner,"
the man replied. "But I know this: I was blind, and now I can
see!" "But what did He do?" they asked. "How did He heal you?"
"Look!" the man exclaimed. "I told you once. Didn't you listen?
Why do you want to hear it again? Do you want to become His
disciples, too?" Then they cursed him and said, "You are His
disciple, but we are disciples of Moses! We know God spoke to

Moses, but we don't even know where this man comes from."
"Why, that's very strange!" the man replied. "He healed my eyes,
and yet you don't know where He comes from?" (John 9:23–30)

The man was seeing clearer than he ever had. He saw who Jesus was. His spiritual eyes had just opened.

"We know that God doesn't listen to sinners, but He is ready
to hear those who worship Him and do His will. Ever since the
world began, no one has been able to open the eyes of someone
born blind. If this man were not from God, He couldn't have
done it." "You were born a total sinner!" they answered. "Are you
trying to teach us?" And they threw him out of the synagogue.
(John 9:31–34)

The very first time the healed man was allowed in the synagogue, the Pharisees threw him out. Before, he was accused of being a sinner because of his blindness, and now he was accused of being a sinner because of his sight. He would never be allowed to worship in the synagogue. But his eyes were now open.

When Jesus heard what had happened, He found the man and
asked, "Do you believe in the Son of Man?" The man answered,
"Who is He, sir? I want to believe in Him." "You have seen Him,"
Jesus said, "and He is speaking to you!" "Yes, Lord, I believe!" the
man said. And he worshiped Jesus. (John 9:35–38)

I am so glad Jesus found him. Jesus heard all that had happened and now needed to help this man see in a new way. "Look right here and see the Messiah," I believe are the words that opened the healed man's eyes. He worshiped Jesus. Blindness was both healed and discovered in this story.

Then Jesus told him, "I entered this world to render judgment— to give sight to the blind and to show those who think they see that they are blind." Some Pharisees who were standing nearby heard Him and asked, "Are You saying we're blind?" (John 9:39-40)

Jesus called them out, and they knew it. If they would open their eyes, they would reach out and touch Him. They would let Him heal their blindness.

"If you were blind, you wouldn't be guilty," Jesus replied. "But you remain guilty because you claim you can see." (John 9:41)

The worst blindness is the kind you don't know you have. In leadership, you will help some people see and discover that some never will see. It is our job to reach out to both kinds of people.

BLIND TO THE FUTURE

Recently, I was invited to a friend's fiftieth birthday party. I didn't think I would be able to attend; it was on a Sunday, and I usually find myself exhausted after preaching three services. But this was a close friend who had moved away and was in town for the occasion, so if there was a way I could do it, I wanted to be there. My energy was better than normal this particular Sunday, so my wife and I ended up going. When we arrived at the restaurant, the party was already in progress. As I walked in, even though I felt an instant connection with many of the guests there, the room got silent. In a sense, I felt eyes of judgment from a few in the room.

I was surrounded by the very people who had helped me start the church—some were from the original group; others had joined our efforts a short time later. Two couples out of the original five were at the party. All the people there were my old neighbors; only one couple still lives in the neighborhood. They were all surprised to see me, and I was surprised to see them. When I started the church, all the experts said, "You will not keep those who start the church with you." That seemed incomprehensible. These were my friends: I had cried with them, prayed with them, and invested in them—and they had invested in me. I couldn't imagine it. How could they leave me? What would make them go? It was impossible for me to understand. So I just tucked that feedback away, not thinking it would apply to me.

One by one, the members of the core group moved away or were upset with the new direction of the church or a decision that was made. Sometimes, something in the service upset them. The two couples at the party who were from the original group no longer attend Gold Creek. The Italian Catholic couple is active at a church down the road, with both their kids in ministry. I am so happy for them. They had promised to help me for a few months and stayed for fifteen years. My converted atheist friend is still following God and has moved thirty miles away. The family is active in their church, and I am friends with the kids. He and his wife stayed with us for fifteen years, and he worked on staff for a brief period of time.

The room was filled with others who had come shortly after we started Gold Creek. Some of those in the room were very uncomfortable with my presence. To me, they felt a little like Pharisees, just remaining in the background. They still harbored some hard feelings toward me for things that had been out of my control. Their words of judgment had stung me when they left. But at that moment, it didn't matter to me what they felt; I was overcome with thanksgiving for each one of them. These were my long-time friends; I really loved them. We shared a rich history together.

Finally, though, someone stood and said what seemed to be on everyone's mind: "I miss the old days of Gold Creek."

Instantly, the reminiscing and teasing began. We were back in the days of camping together, setting up an elementary school gym, planning services, and serving together. The memories poured out. Each one brought a smile, and any feelings of remorse or hurt were lost in the moment. The memories were good, and we celebrated and recalled some amazing days. One friend stopped to thank me for bringing this group of friends together.

But I couldn't help but think two things. First, they were good days—not easy days—but good days. I said that out loud. Many agreed, and we remembered all the sacrifices that went into the early days of starting the church. With every change and every decision, someone would become blind to what we were doing. As a leader, my job is often to step toward pain, even when I see it coming. Through the years, I have felt the pain of growing with Gold Creek. The pain I felt was the loss of those friends and relationships in order to lead in the direction God was calling us.

But, the other thing, I left unsaid: I don't long for the good old days of Gold Creek—the best days are right now. The best is yet to come! God is always doing new things—this is His church, not ours. His plans are bigger than I am. His plans are bigger than our memories.

Sometimes our blindness happens because we are looking backward, instead of forward. When we see only our past, we can't see our future. Our vision has to be continually examined by our Maker, so that we don't become blind like the Pharisees.

QUESTIONS TO THINK ABOUT

1. What do you have trouble seeing?

2. What are the big questions that have you stuck?

3. Who are you in this story?
   a. The disciples with the big why?
   b. The blind man with an impossible problem?
   c. The Pharisees unable to see God's power in front of them?
   d. The parents who are so afraid of Pharisees that they become blind like them?

4. Do you have a story of your eyes being opened?

5. What kind of pain have you felt as a leader because of the blindness of others?

6. What kind of vision does God have for your future?

7. Is the future brighter than the past?

8. What would it take to open your eyes?

Eight

The Pharisees in Our Culture

We stand at the edge of a road right alongside the dump, watching bears devour their meals. Suddenly, the wind shifts, and the scents of my family waft to the bears. In an instant, every bear is running at top speed. Two of them head right for my wife, my ten-year-old son, my six-year-old daughter, and me. It happens so fast, there's nothing we can do. I scream my instructions and hope for the best.

DANGER AT THE DUMP

Audrey and I had some dear friends, Mason and Jewel, in Willits, California. We lived in Concord, California—a place crowded with people—and needed a break from the city. So we packed up our kids, Daniel and Kristen, and drove up to visit our friends. I love visiting the woods of coastal Northern California—the redwood groves are spectacular. At the end of our first day there, Mason and Jewel told us they had a treat in store. They planned to take us to look at the local wildlife. We all piled into Mason's car and headed to a surprise destination. He told us on the way that he'd found a spot for us to look at bears. Apparently, the local dump attracted big California black bears, so we were going to check it out.

I thought about my first experience viewing the bears with my dad in Stehekin, Washington, and couldn't wait for my kids to enjoy a little excitement from the safety of the car. With a chuckle of anticipation, Mason described the last time he took his family there. It was going to be a blast.

When we drove up to the dump, the gate was closed. Not to be deterred, Mason got out and tried to open it. No luck. There was no way to see the bears. I don't remember if it was his idea or mine, but we decided it might be okay to go around the gate and walk up the road to look at the bears from a distance. Bears have poor eyesight and will often not even notice a human's presence. I didn't know that the road led right to the dump.

Leaving behind the security and protection of the vehicle, my two kids and all four of us adults started to walk up the road. Since Mason had been there before, I was certain he wouldn't take us on a road that would lead too close to the bears. But he was unfamiliar with bears and only remembered watching from the car. I should have asked more questions.

We walked up the road leading to the top of a hill. When we rounded the corner, I noticed some black tops of bears moving slowly as they rummaged for food fifty yards away. The ripe odors of the recent and not-so-recent piles were pungent. The bears hadn't noticed us, but they were closer than I thought they would be. With a few more steps, they came into full view. Eight bears of all sizes moved around, intently digging for their dinner.

My kids were amazed and excited to see the bears— it was like a real-life trip to the zoo. We whispered so the bears wouldn't notice us. It

Bears digging through a dump, like the one we visited.

was exhilarating to be so close. They looked harmless and appeared to be distracted. Suddenly, the wind shifted. One of the bears caught our scent and bolted away. His movement alerted the others, and they moved at what seemed like warp speed. I wondered if the smell of humans was more appetizing than garbage.

Two bears headed right for us. It took the bears one second to close the gap. *What do I do?* I thought. My two kids and my wife stood frozen, watching the bears. Who would I save? It was a good thing I didn't have too much time to think about it. All I could yell was "Spread out—they can't get us all!" The two bears ran right between all of us, passing by at less than three feet.

We scrambled down the hill as fast as we could, away from the bears, thankful that none of us was hurt. I will never forget how fast it happened and how dangerous it was for my kids. I was not sure it was really worth it.

I wanted my kids to have an adventure, but I would not have intentionally put them in such a dangerous position. Yet sometimes when we join the adventure of following Jesus, there is no guarantee that it will be safe for us—or for our families. Quite simply, following Jesus is dangerous. So what was His dangerous mission?

JESUS IN HIS HOMETOWN

"The Spirit of the LORD is upon Me, for He has anointed Me to bring Good News to the poor. He has sent Me to proclaim that captives will be released, that the blind will see, that the oppressed will be set free, and that the time of the LORD's favor has come." He rolled up the scroll, handed it back to the attendant, and sat down. All eyes in the synagogue looked at Him intently. Then He began to speak to them. "The Scripture you've just heard has been fulfilled this very day!" (Luke 4:18-21)

Jesus was in His hometown synagogue. He had been living there in Nazareth for thirty years, listening to the reading of the Scripture. I am sure He had attended the synagogue weekly and knew every face there that day, even those of the local Pharisees. To our knowledge, He had never had a run-in with anyone. He was a well-respected carpenter who ran Joseph's shop. We don't know what had happened to his father, but most scholars believe that His dad had died. Jesus had recently been baptized by John and begun His work as a rabbi. On this particular day, He was there as the new rabbi, with His disciples in tow. The expectations of Him from His hometown crowd were low.

Everyone spoke well of Him and was amazed by the gracious words that came from His lips. "How can this be?" they asked. "Isn't this Joseph's son?" (Luke 4:22)

He was known not as Jesus, but as Joseph's son. His reputation was good, but were the people ready for His words? Notice that everyone spoke well of Him. I am convinced that is the point of danger: when you know something is about to change.

Then He said, "You will undoubtedly quote Me this proverb: 'Physician, heal yourself'—meaning, 'Do miracles here in Your hometown like those You did in Capernaum.' But I tell you the truth, no prophet is accepted in His own hometown. (Luke 4:23–24)

I can understand my not being accepted in my hometown, but Jesus? This man was perfect. Never had any young man in that town lived a life any purer than Jesus.

That would not be the problem I would have. Any number of kids could point at me and tell some story of what I was like as a child. My messages lose some of their punch because of me, but not because of Jesus.

Jesus's problem was what He knew about people. They couldn't accept Him because He knew them. I am sure they expected Jesus to be like every other Pharisee or rabbi. He would have been full of judgment. I am not sure they could have heard the message of John 3:17:

God sent His Son into the world not to judge the world, but to save the world through Him.

In order to accept grace, you have to admit you need it. Let's get back to Jesus in His hometown synagogue.

"Certainly there were many needy widows in Israel in Elijah's time, when the heavens were closed for three and a half years, and a severe famine devastated the land. Yet Elijah was not sent to any of them. He was sent instead to a foreigner—a widow of Zarephath in the land of Sidon. And there were many lepers in Israel in the time of the prophet Elisha, but the only one healed was Naaman, a Syrian." (Luke 4:25-27)

Jesus was telling the people that He would not spend any time there. He was really saying that they were no better than the Gentiles, so He would be going elsewhere. He knew them well, and they thought they knew Him well. It was a bold and dangerous move for Him to expose the hypocrisy in His own hometown.

When they heard this, the people in the synagogue were furious. (Luke 4:28)

I am always amazed at how quickly a crowd can turn against you. It doesn't seem that Jesus's words warranted that much reaction.

Jumping up, they mobbed Him and forced Him to the edge of the hill on which the town was built. They intended to push Him over the cliff. (Luke 4:29)

Jesus had led His disciples into a mob. His old friends and synagogue leaders, along with the local Pharisees, charged Him and were ready to kill Him. His ministry had just begun, but they wanted to finish it before it started.

The leadership adventure God calls us to is bold and dangerous. At times, it seems that disaster is imminent. I suspect the disciples that day tried to control the mob, to no avail.

But He passed right through the crowd and went on His way. (Luke 4:30)

If you ever wondered if Jesus was a girly-guy, wonder no more. Enough was enough. He walked through them. Not around them, not away from them, no, he walked *through* them. Samson had nothing on Jesus that day. Years of carpentry had prepared Him to lead through this danger. No wonder men were following Jesus; they recognized a man who was not afraid to rumble when the time was right. They would eventually take His life, but in reality, Jesus gave up His life so that we would not be afraid of the danger we might face. Someday, we may be called to give up our lives in this leadership adventure, but that will only be in His timing. When He leads me, I have all the power I need to face my danger.

TAKING A LOOK AT TODAY'S CULTURE

The year 2014 has been one in which I've seen our culture take a huge step away from its Christian roots. We have lost the battle in our country. One day my kids, who are both in ministry, will be led to a place of danger. The Pharisees of this day are insisting that we accept a new morality or else. Everyday some new court case comes down demanding that I give up my right to believe the way I do. Our culture takes our Scriptures and tells us how we must interpret them or we are bigots. Each day sees another headline of someone else who is being bullied by a new agenda. The legislature in California took five minutes to pass a law that allows children who are "confused about their sexual identity" to go to whichever locker room they want. Now, it is law in California that our girls or boys who shower after a soccer game cannot be protected from a confused child of the opposite sex who may shower at the same time. If we say anything about it, we are bigots.

The courts in Utah now allow for multiple marriages. We only have to look at Rome to see what is coming next. It will be scary and dangerous for our kids to be genuine followers of Jesus. When we encourage our kids to follow Jesus, we invite persecution and ridicule to come their way. The only discrimination allowed now is for genuine followers of Jesus. We are walking into a dangerous place to lead. It is our own country.

So what do we do?

We learn from Jesus. This is exactly what Jesus led His disciples into. The disciples walked into a culture full of people who hated them, and yet they changed the world. The disciples lived under the rule of Rome, which burned Christians to light the night sky. Their own Jewish leaders hunted them down. They were beaten, tortured, whipped, and killed. But the great news of Jesus marched on. This little band of twelve now has the largest following in the world. That is leadership!

I know what needs to happen. We need Jesus's leadership in our lives so we can lead our families, our businesses, our churches, and our country. Is it safe? Not really. Is it worth it? Absolutely! Our world is looking for truth that satisfies. Our culture says nothing is really a sin. Our culture says God would never allow you to go to Hell. But God's truth says He sent His son to save us from ourselves. Hell is ours only if we want it to be. When we live our lives as far away from God as we can, then God will give us our wish for eternity. Our culture is hungry for God's truth. People will follow when we provide some genuine leadership. Instead of being silent, we need to lead. We need to put aside our fears and follow Jesus as He leads us in a new direction.

HOW TO CHANGE AN ATHEIST

My brother Ron and I went on a mule-deer hunting trip into Idaho. We'd planned a two-week adventure by horseback into the high country in the southwest part of the state. I arrived late and had to hike the ten miles into the camp that was already set up. When I got there, I stepped into a conflict already in motion.

My brother's friend John had invited his horse-riding buddy Sam to join us. Sam owned the main tent with the wood stove and all the kitchen gear. It was cold and snowy; the only way to get warm was to join Sam in his tent. I discovered shortly after I got there that Sam was creating quite a stir. He was not shy about his beliefs: he was an atheist, a nudist, and an anti-hunter. Why in the world would an anti-hunter agree to go on a hunting trip? Sam is the Pharisee that says, "Believe my way or else." I think the problem is clear.

Ron chose to spend his time in the unheated tent with our friend John. Nobody liked Sam, but we needed to eat in his tent. Plus, he would be with us for the entire two weeks. We could not get away from him. I wonder what Sam felt when I, the preacher, showed up.

I walked into his tent at dinnertime. The discussion around the table was already heated. Within the first ten minutes, Sam confronted me. He made fun of me, deriding me for my belief in a fairytale called the Bible and its main character, God. Sam tried to pick a fight by describing my beliefs with language that reduced my manhood. My brother rolled his eyes and left the tent. He was furious that we would be spending two weeks with this guy.

Over the years, I have learned to respect anyone who is honest with his or her beliefs. I love to talk with atheists because they are so sure there is no God and that's all they want to talk about. They are good people, and they are sure they have the answer. What they cannot debate, though, is the presence of God in us. When we show up, God shows up. I don't remember all I said that night, but I tried to listen and befriend Sam. I think God gives us words that we don't even know we have. Sam began to tolerate me.

The next morning, the hunting started. My brother and John decided that the two best people to hunt together would be the preacher and the atheist. It was shaping up to be an interesting day. Before we split up, we spotted some monster mule deer on the hill about two miles away. We watched them bed down, so we set a path to get close to them. I could not understand why Sam, an anti-hunter, was on a hunting trip. But here we were, drawing straws to see who would shoot first, and Sam wanted to be part of it. Again, my brother rolled his eyes. Ron won the draw, so off we went up the hill.

We were on horseback traveling without a trail up a mountainside that was steep and covered with loose shale. My horse got scared on the way up the mountain. It was obvious to John, the owner of the horse, that I would soon be bucked off. He yelled at me to dismount. I chose to dismount on the usual side, the left, but that was the downhill side. I was halfway off when the horse bucked and flipped me head over heels down the steep hill. One and a half turns later, I landed on my right shoulder, and the side of my face. I was injured. Nothing was broken,

Still smiling after my tumble down the hill.

but I knew I had really hurt my shoulder, and it would make the rest of the trip very difficult.

After a few minutes, I was back on the horse and riding again. We never found those deer. Much to the relief of all of us, Sam decided to go back to camp. We rode another twelve miles that day through the high country. It was beautiful! We saw elk in rut in every draw. On the way back to camp, I spotted a mule deer and harvested it. It was getting dark, so we cleaned the deer and left it to be picked up the next morning.

When we arrived back at camp, Sam was at his best. He was ready to argue all his beliefs. First on the agenda was politics, then God, followed by nudism and hunting. Ron left early, but I stayed and listened and talked.

The next day, Sam was again assigned to partner up with me to go and retrieve the deer. We each had a packhorse to help carry the deer back to camp. My shoulder injury had made it impossible to sleep, and it was a long ride. I was injured and hurting—and stuck with Sam.

After a four-hour ride, we finally got to the deer. As we loaded it, Sam informed me that he might just shoot a deer if we saw one. Seizing the opportunity, and with nothing to lose, I asked Sam if I could pray that God would help us find a deer on the way back. He laughed and ridiculed me, but I prayed out loud anyway.

We hadn't traveled more than thirty minutes when, right in front of us, a buck stood on the trail. I stopped the horses and helped Sam get in position to shoot. As he shot, the horses tried to run, and my injured shoulder was put to the test. After the dust cleared, I realized Sam had missed an easy one-hundred-yard shot. I laughed to myself, thinking that God was having fun with him. As we got on the horses, I reminded Sam of my prayer. What did I have to lose? He quickly dismissed it as just a coincidence. So I prayed out loud again: "Lord, it would be great if you could help Sam get his first deer." Ten minutes later, that same deer ended up on the trail in front of us. Sam got off his horse, aimed, and shot the deer. I celebrated with Sam as he harvested his first deer. I taught him how to clean it. I waited, but Sam never said anything about God. So I did. "Sam, I need to thank God for providing you with this deer." I said a prayer of thanks, and Sam was quiet.

That night, dinner was non-confrontational, as a true miracle had happened: an anti-hunter had harvested his first deer. The next day, my shoulder was worse, and I had to leave camp. Sam volunteered to help me pack out. We loaded up and made it to the vehicles. Sam wanted to go into town with me, so he followed me to a restaurant. We celebrated with a burger. As we ate, Sam shared his story. He admitted that he had never had anyone explain God to him as I had. He cried and opened his heart up to Jesus at a greasy burger joint. I'd left early because of my injury, but Sam went back to finish the trip with Ron and John. I received a phone call from my brother when he got out of the woods.

"What did you say to Sam?" Ron asked.

Sam was a changed man.

I don't know what happened to Sam after our encounter; I just know he genuinely met God. I am convinced that if God can change Sam, He can change anyone. The key for each of us is to be in genuine relationship with someone who needs God.

Jesus's plan to change the world is easy. I am responsible to introduce God to those around me. Our culture doesn't know God. If it did, the people would follow Him. He always has our best interests in mind. He is what we need and long for in our souls. Jesus is what the people in our culture are looking for, even if they don't know it. God has called us to lead in a time such as this. Our culture is hungry for the truth we have. If the people today genuinely meet Jesus, they will follow.

QUESTIONS TO THINK ABOUT

1. What are the changes in our culture that have you most alarmed?

2. What happens when you try to talk about these issues?

3. Who of those you know is meeting God for the first time through you?

4. What can you do to help control your emotions and listen to another point of view?

5. Who is someone in your life you are leading toward truth?

6. Who would be a miracle if he or she converted?

7. Is God calling you to pray for that person?

8. Are you willing to face the danger of our culture?

9. Are you willing to lead your family into this danger?

Conclusion

It's the second-largest island in the United States: Kodiak Island, Alaska. On the south coast of Alaska, it's home to a species of bears all their own—Kodiak bears. They are huge—the only other bears that match their size are polar bears. The males average one thousand pounds, and large males weigh up to 1,500 pounds. Their average height at the shoulders is four feet, with larger bears towering at five feet tall. Their length can be between eight and ten feet. The population of these bears is managed through hunting. Trophy hunters harvest about 180 bears each year. There are 3,500 bears there—a density of almost one bear per square mile. That's a lot of bears on a small island. Many bears will live and die on this island without being disturbed by a human. There are new record-sized bears being harvested every year.

There is also a large population of deer on the island. Hunters go into the field to harvest them every year and encounter bears. Because of those encounters, every other year, on average, there are bear attacks that end in severe maulings. It is definitely a place that gets your heart pumping when you go for a walk in the wilderness.

I want to meet one of those Kodiak bears, one of those monsters in the wild. I love that kind of adventure. When I spoke at my son's church and presented the material for this book, the congregation gave me an offering to start a fund for an adventure of a lifetime. I want that to be a Kodiak-bear adventure.

I believe the best days are ahead for me. I am on the adventure of a lifetime right now. Leadership challenges are stretching me and helping me grow. God's call in my life is as strong as ever. I am not done yet. I hope the biggest bears are behind me. But I know there are still bears to watch out for.

Right before Jesus left this earth, He gave us this challenge.

Therefore, go and make disciples of all the nations, baptizing them in the name of the Father and the Son and the Holy Spirit. (Matthew 28:19)

That is our leadership adventure! God is calling us to go anywhere and everywhere. Open your eyes to the adventure. He needs us to go. It doesn't matter how old you are or if you have it all together. He says go. This is *your* adventure of a lifetime.

I think you will want to go. So, here are some things you're going to need in order to accept the challenge and go on this adventure.

Courage. It is the ability to step out, move forward, and hold your ground, in spite of your fear. It is not the absence of fear. You would have to be partially crazy not to see the danger in our culture. Leadership is scary, but courage steps into that fear.

Discipline. It is so easy to lose our way and follow a rabbit trail that takes us away from our leadership challenge. There are lots of good things in this world that can keep us from our path. Discipline keeps us at the task. We need discipline in our personal lives as well. Seventy percent of all pastors who start do not finish. It is the lack of discipline that often does them in. You are no different from a pastor. Recognize your strengths and weaknesses and develop a good plan to use them both to your advantage. Discipline will help you stay on the path.

Direction. You need this to help set your course. There is nothing that takes the place of a daily quiet time so you can listen for direction. When I get going too fast, I forget to look for direction. For the last ten years, I have developed the habit of reading the *One Year Bible* daily. It is a great reminder of the many leaders and the paths they have taken. Some of them lost their way. Others, who were incredibly lost, found a direction and helped others do the same. I don't think there is a day that I don't gain direction from my daily devotional times.

Team. I have never liked to go into the woods alone. When I get in trouble, I want others there with me to advise me. In the leadership game, you need some people on the inside. Usually, it's a trusted family member or co-worker. And you also need some on the outside. I have learned that others see me more clearly than I see myself. My team members have saved me more than once—and I have been involved in saving them.

Resources. When I am at the end of my resources—and at the end of myself—that is when God does His best work. It is at this point I am reminded that I am on His mission—I have His resources. I don't have because I don't ask.

"Teach these new disciples to obey all the commands I have given you. And be sure of this: I am with you always, even to the end of the age." (Matthew 28:20)

Most important, you need **God**. His challenge for us is never something we can do on our own. Only God can accomplish what He has called you into.

I pray that God will use this book as you join Him for an adventure in leadership—and watch out for bears.